GW00544430

Letter to a New Grandson

The Story of a WW2 Lancaster Pilot

Wally Kasper

Snow Wolf Press
Pat Cher Books
patcherbooks@gmail.com

Cover, Sky Photograph, Garry Fancy
Cover, Lancaster Bomber painting, Mary
Cher

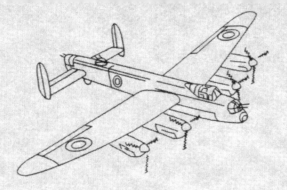

Dear Dad,

The arrival of your first grandson, two weeks ago, just reaffirms my earlier request to you to take the time to set down some kind of an outline of the things that happened to you during the war years.

During our early twenties we were busy with our university studies and enjoying life in Canada even though the studies were hard. During your twenties you were far away in another country busy with the unpleasantness of war.

We have never heard any of those experiences and I'm sure that in the years to come my children will be as curious as I am about those days and that part of Canadian history - about that we seem to know so little.

Would you please take the time and write for us an outline of those experiences so that in the years to come we will have a better understanding of that history and of you.

Love,

Jennifer

Nepean, Ontario

Dear Kyle,

This project began when you were just one month old. It does seem a bit strange to be writing a letter to a person who will not read it until twenty or so years later. As you enter your final high school years, or university, I hope you will be curious about the history of the land you live in and the times and the events that preceded your period.

Each generation makes its own contribution to their time and deals with the problems that arise. One of the terrible events of my generation was what history describes as World War II.

The cost of this war to the many nations involved was beyond anyone's capacity to calculate, and, in terms of the lives that were sacrificed, the contributions that those people could have made is beyond anyone's imagining.

One of those lives was my older brother, Russell. He was in the Canadian Army and was killed in northern France in August of 1944. His infantry regiment had been part of the British Canadian invasion forces that had opened up one of the Normandy sectors.

8

By August of 1944 they had moved eastward behind the retreating German Army and had come to a place called Neufchateau. It had been a headquarters for the German army and had an orchard on its grounds.

When the Germans left they placed land mines in the orchard grounds, and one evening Russell stepped on one of them.

My wartime years were spend in the Royal Canadian Air Force. The time spent on 408 Bomber Squadron is the subject matter of the following Tour Diary.

I hope that this Diary will give you some small appreciation for that unpleasant part of my life, and, most of all, I hope that the ebb or flood tides of war will never sweep across the land in that you live.

With much love and every good wish.

Your Grandfather.

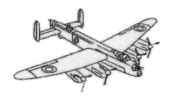

"The Bomber Offensive was the most continuous and the most gruelling operation of war ever carried out. It lasted for some 2000 days and nights and served as the only effective weapon at the throat of Hitler's Germany for four years."

British Official History of The War

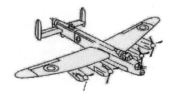

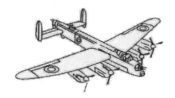

Tour Diary
Preliminaries

Many months prior to my arrival at Bomber Squadron, my first Air Force steps brought me to the Royal Canadian Air Force Manning Depot in Edmonton, Alberta.

The long-suffering drill corporals were the birth pangs that turned us into airmen with pressed pants, shiny boots and with an attitude fit for presentation to the public. They taught us that we had a right and a left foot, and how to distinguish between the two. We were given uniforms and inoculations, and soon sent on our way to start the serious business of learning to fly.

The drill Corporal assigned to act as house-mother to flight trainees told us repeatedly, that the standards of dress and appearance, deemed to be excellent or better for civilians, would be normal or standard for us.

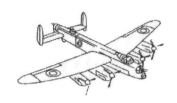

And so it was, and, even at this late date in our lives, you can meet ex-airmen who reflexively keep their shoes shined and their pants pressed as they learned to do as raw recruits, perhaps not to the same level of spit and polish, but certainly respectable.

We were proud and polished airmen on the day we were given the small white flashes that we put into the front of our wedge hats to denote that we were now flight cadets, on our way to learn to fly.

The Initial Training School (ITS) in Regina, Saskatchewan, was calling. We took the train ride from Edmonton in stride. It was the first stage towards the day we would get our pilot's wings. My horizons didn't go much farther than that.

ITS was all ground school work. We had a number of Americans in the school (the United States was not yet in the war), and a few trainees who had been out of high school for some time and needed a refresher on their high school physics. All needed to learn something about the theory of flight, about meteorology and so on.

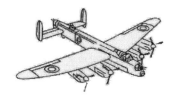

The Station Commander just loved to show off the Boys in Blue to the local people of the city so every Sunday morning we did a five mile route march around the town. My memories of Regina are a jumble of cold sunny Sunday mornings and blistered feet.

We eagerly awaited our next training phase, Elementary Flying Training School (EFTS). There were four Canadians and twenty Americans in the course, and we had only to move across the city to the grass field aerodrome that had been built there.

The first sight of the rows of Tiger Moth biplanes brought a new excitement to our lives. The great day was really here.

We dug into the half-day ground school, half day flying training routine, and were soon on our way to learning the 'circuits and bumps' facts of life.

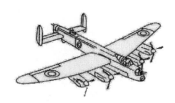

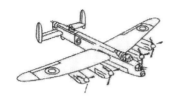

You learned to position yourself and the aircraft into the wind at one end of the grass field and then with full throttle the aircraft started its journey down the field, reached takeoff speed, and climbed away into the sky.

It took a couple of takeoffs to get the whole process sorted out in your mind, until you felt at ease with it, but even at this distance in time, it is easy to remember the excitement of those first flights.

We would fly away a short distance and then come back to the aerodrome, learn to enter the circuit (the controlled area above the aerodrome from which you made your approaches) and come in and land. The landings were the 'bumps' part of the 'circuit and bumps' but you soon learned to keep them below crash level.

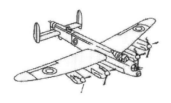

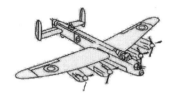

After eight hours of instruction that included a few short introductions to aerobatics, I was sent on my first solo flight. Just one circuit and a bump or two, and then still alive, with an intact aircraft, I took the plane back to the flight line and received the applause of my fellow cadets.

After that, the solo training exercises began in earnest. These were happy hours of being out in the clear morning sunshine doing various exercises and always throwing in a number of loops and rolls. When the weatherman was kind enough to provide some cumulus clouds to play with, a bit of 'cloud hopping' would be on the menu. It is hard to describe the sense of freedom and excitement that each solo session brought.

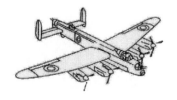

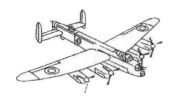

Years later, I read John Gillespie Magee Jr.'s poem, 'High Flight,

*"Oh I have slipped the surly bonds of earth,
And danced the skies on laughter silvered wings".*

The words resonated with the unspoken feelings that flooded through my mind on those joyful mornings. It happened again, years later, when I found myself taking a few familiarization flights in a Spitfire, and again, when I found myself in an F-86 Sabre jet. The experience is impossible to capture in words.

All too soon our time on the venerable Tiger Moth was over and we were off on the next stage of our flying training.

Of course everyone was hoping to be sent to a single engine secondary training school instead of a twin engine one, because it would mean we could go overseas to fly Spitfires.

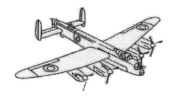

Twin engine training meant forgetting the dream of someday flying Spitfires.

We swallowed hard when the postings were announced, and stood silently while our dreams of Spitfire glory vanished from our hearts and minds. I remember clearly telling myself that my wings were still waiting for me and there was much adventure ahead.

But war has its own needs and its own logic, and we went to Claresholm, Alberta, where they were flying the Cessna Crane, at 15 Service Flying Training School (SFTS).

Our broken hearts soon mended as the Crane was a fine aircraft, a very stable, student-friendly aircraft, and most of us soon developed a love affair with the splendid yellow bird.

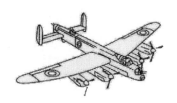

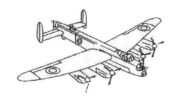

We were within viewing distance of the foothills of the Rockies and the temptation to go a bit closer was great. We were told that there were curious downdrafts from the mountains that could be dangerous and that flying in that region was forbidden.

The point was all too graphically brought home when one of our more adventurous fellows went out into the forbidden area and it turned out to be his last trip.

The funeral vividly etched in my mind the idea that rules were sensible and made to protect us.

There was a lot of emphasis on aerial navigation and we had to do exercises in that one of us would fly and one of us would navigate. We soon settled into an easy relationship with our flying buddies and learned a bit about the vast complexities of aerial navigation.

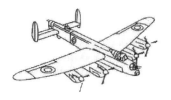

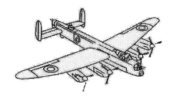

The night trips were a bit of a menace for when we were navigating we had to take star shots on a bubble sextant. For some reason a sextant seemed to be able to mesmerize me into producing position points that were always on another continent.

In later years, when I learned of the advent of the American Ground Positioning System (GPS), I remember having far too many scotches, one evening, with a navigator friend of mine, and celebrating the passing into history of the sextant. No fond memories there.

Suddenly, it seemed, wings parade day was looming large on our horizons. We had lost a few of our course mates as 'wash-outs' and were very sorry to see them leave us to go to some uncertain future.

All in all there had been a great deal of hard work and dedication not to mention the cost of the whole program to the Canadian taxpayer.

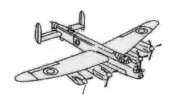

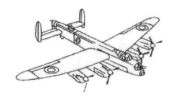

Imagine, if you will, a huge training base, kitchens, hospital, classrooms, fire trucks and the thousands of things needed to make the whole process work, just to give someone like me some hours of flying time in a Cessna Crane.

Wars are never cheap.

We didn't think of it at the time, but we would not begin to pay for ourselves, as an economic unit (a pilot) until we were flying a Lancaster bomber half a world away from the foothills at Claresholm. There would still be many more costs in our training before the day we flew a first mission on a bomber squadron.

Pilots were a rather expensive commodity.

Wings Parade excitement buzzed through the barracks, and then we were finished all the flying exercises, had our flying tests with the testing officer, and pronounced fit to be given our pilots wings.

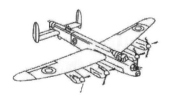

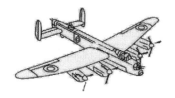

The weatherman had been speaking to God so we had a spectacular bright, sunny, Alberta morning. We stepped out and the Chief Flying Instructor pinned our wings on our tunics. We emerged, like a butterfly from a cocoon, to have a new beauty, or so it seemed, when we saw the young ladies looking at us.

Our postings, to the next step, in our respective odysseys during those dark years, came with our wings, mine to take me to the General Reconnaissance School in Summerside, Prince Edward Island, where I would enter the Specialist Navigators training program and be taught all the magical things that navigators learned.

The Royal Air Force Coastal Command had evolved a system whereby they took three pilots for their long range aircraft, pilots who had had special navigator's training, one to fly for a couple of hours, one to navigate, and one to sleep or make coffee. Thus, no need for extra bodies who were only navigators.

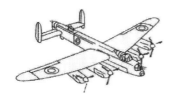

Months later when I was immersed in the bomber command aircrew mix I used to hear the navigators assure us that pilots were just navigators with their brains kicked out, I would smile and acquaint the with the facts of life.

We never had our hands on the controls of a plane at GRS, just sat in the back of an Anson that flew at about one hundred feet above the Atlantic for hours while we did all the exotic plots on charts that navigators do. Daytime flights, night time flights, star shots ad infinitum, and all of this in the cold winter months. The Anson never made the heating hall of fame.

There was one small extra that befell me. Whenever I was seated beyond the centre of gravity in these Ansons, flying at these low heights over the water in the cold weather (the flights were always bumpy), I was invariably airsick.

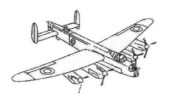

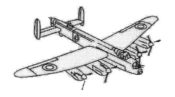

So, I carried my barf-can in my navigator's bag of tricks. The pilots never noticed, as long as the aircraft was clean. If they had, I'm sure I would have been washed out of the course. It must have been a common enough reaction among the students.

When we completed the course, we asked if we were allowed to wear both the pilot and navigator wings but were told that it would look unbalanced on our uniforms.

Two weeks of embarkation leave at home and then back to Halifax. A quick, overnight train trip to New York, and then we marched right on the Queen Mary. It set a record for its crossing time, after a submarine scare shortly after we left the harbour.

The ship zigzagged at 17 knots all the way across the Atlantic and everyone aboard, excepting some crew members, was sea-sick.

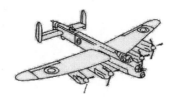

WINGS PARADE

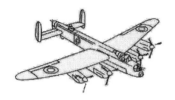

The ship was packed, with soldiers, sailors and airmen tucked into every conceivable space. Words cannot describe the trip. If Dante had been alive I'm sure he would have included it in his Inferno.

At Gourock, Scotland the boys in blue marched off the ship onto a waiting train that took us to Bournemouth. It turned out to be a lovely south coast holiday playground with many hotels. It was ideal, for temporary accommodation for Canadians and a sprinkling of our colonial cousins, the Australians and New Zealanders.

The military processes, like the Mills of God, grind slowly, but they grind exceedingly small. It took the personal files of each man about five months to catch up. My file would, of course, have told the personnel people that I was anointed by the Personnel Gods of the Royal Canadian Air Force Headquarters and sent off to
Coastal Command.

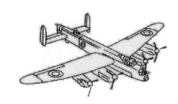

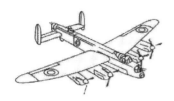

Now, it just so happened that I had three cousins who had been serving for some time in Coastal Command. Their correspondence indicated that they felt they had the most boring jobs on the face of the globe with endless hours flying over the ocean seeing nothing but wave tops. One of them later went missing.

When we arrived at Bournemouth, the Air Force authorities, not having our personal files, and no information at all on us, gave us a form to fill out. The usual name, rank number, and in the upper left and corner of the sheet, and then you were asked to fill in your first, second and third choices for postings.

My old buddy from Summerside days, Don McCrae, and I looked at each other, and then, with tongue in cheek, we put down Bomber Command as our first, second and third choices. Unknown to us, Bomber Command had been savaged as the Germans improved their radar and defenses, and they badly needed aircrew to replace the heavy losses they had been sustaining.

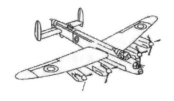

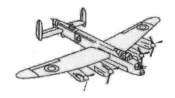

Don and I were out of Bournemouth three days later on the next step of our training.

Coastal Command, fare thee well.

Don went to a flying refresher course, (remember we had been away from piloting for some time now) and I to a two month course up on the west coast cliffs, looking out at the North Sea, where we were given a course in 'unarmed combat'.

Unlike the Americans we did not carry sidearms, so if we were forced to bail out over enemy territory and were confronted by a German soldier with a rifle and bayonet, we had no defences. We were taught the fine art of how to deal with him.

Our Royal Marine instructors were the toughest bunch of men I have ever seen and their pedagogy was to inflict learning by the experience of pain. The Royal Marines had been doing this kind of thing for a couple of hundred years. I'm sure they thought we were the saddest group of 'soldiers' they had ever seen.

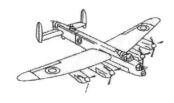

Throughout this tough course I kept one thing uppermost in my mind--none of them had ever flown an aircraft. These were the longest and most painful months of my life, and our last day on that course was one of the most welcome.

But it was here, in Sunderland County, that I met the girl with the Red-Red Hair. More of this later.

Back to Bournemouth, and the next day I was on my way to the flying training program that would take me to the front doors of Bomber Command.

They certainly did not waste a moment getting us on our way; conversion to a new aircraft, lots of night flying practice, and shortly on to Operational Training Unit on Wellington aircraft.

I picked up my crew and we learned to work together as a group, and got down to the serious business of preparation for our days at bomber squadron.

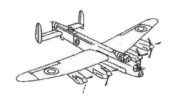

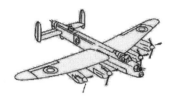

Circuits and bumps, day flying, night flying and cross country trips to get all the crew members fine tuned were the order of the day. Quite a lot of fine-tuning was required. On our first night cross country trip we were scheduled to go from our base in the Midlands to Dublin, to the Orkney Islands and then back to base. All this flying was at 15,000 feet, so we could get familiar with the cold and the use of oxygen.

Ireland was a neutral nation during the war so we dare not overfly but since there was no blackout we could use the lights of the city as a good position indicator. We were expected to turn northeast on our next heading a few miles before we got to the city itself.

Part of the way out on the course to Dublin a pilot would expect the navigator to give him an estimated time of arrival (ETA) for the Dublin turning point as well as the new heading for the
next leg of the trip.

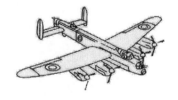

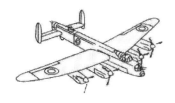

Our navigator was as silent as the Sphinx, and, as Dublin was looming ever larger, I asked him for an ETA and a new course and he said OK. But the silence continued so I turned on the autopilot and went back to his small cubbyhole.

(Note: The Navigator and the Wireless Operator required a light to do their work so they were in a small cubicle that was blacked out with curtains so the light could not be seen from outside.}

He was sitting reading a novel and his chart, that should have had many notations by now, was completely blank.

I quickly calculated a rough new heading for the next leg, and went back to my seat, completed the turn onto the new course, re-set the auto-pilot and went back to the navigator's table and did a rough re-work of the trip from base to get a wind factor and a new ETA for the Orkneys and a heading back to base.

So the trip went with a few quick checks back to the navigators chart as we went along.

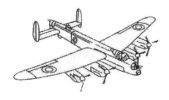

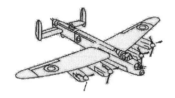

About half way between the Orkneys and base the rear gunner spoke-up on the intercom and told me that he had been watching an aircraft that had been flying parallel to us and a few thousand feet higher. It was too far away for him to identify. We cruised along for a few more minutes and then the gunner said Port Go, our standard warning for an attacking aircraft.

I turned sharply to port in a quick climb and we saw a great burst of tracer from the guns of a Junkers 88 night fighter fly under
the bottom of our aircraft. He knew that we had seen him so he went away seeking other targets of opportunity. I remember being devoutly thankful that I had been sitting in the pilot's seat at that moment instead of at the navigator's desk.

It will come as no surprise that the rest of the crew were somewhat displeased at the navigator's performance. Next morning he
and I took a quick trip to the Chief
Flying Instructor's office.

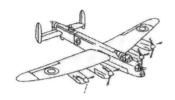

His next stop was an abrupt dismissal from the RCAF in Montreal and mine was to say Hello to a new navigator, a splendid fellow who broke his arm some weeks later falling from his bicycle.

We emerged from that night cross-country trip with a new perspective on our duties. Not yet on the squadron and we had come with a dozen feet of that burst of tracer from the German night fighter. It seemed to be a sobering lesson for all the crews in training there and no one could doubt that, as Sherlock Holmes might have said to Dr. Watson The game is being played in earnest.

We were given a new navigator and the Wing Commander made a wry comment, at our next cross country briefing, on how I might pay a bit more attention to the care and feeding of navigators as they were an expensive commodity.

This one was brilliant, rather quiet, a bit withdrawn, unaccustomed to the banter and easy nonsense of the rest of us.

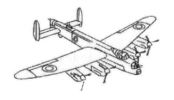

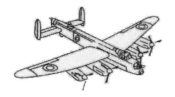

He did not smoke or drink, had never had a date with a girl, but was the squadron's ace navigator, as he proved very quickly after we arrived there.

The navigators on the squadron would meet after a raid and would back plot their charts from the night before. In this way they could determine what all the others had done. It was an excellent learning process for all of them because there were some clever fellows in the crowd.

By the time we had done six trips the Nav leader was using our navigator's chart as the master from that all others were judged. High praise indeed.

We were now well into the training schedule and our next posting was looming large on the horizon. We, as crew, still had to finish the OTL course, and then the quick conversion to the Lancaster, before we were ready to hit the Bomber Squadron.

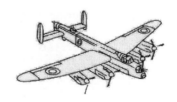

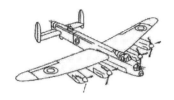

What incredible luck it was that took me to 408 Squadron where they had the Mark 11 Lancasters, (there were only three squadrons of these in all of Bomber Command) at Linton-on-Ouse, eight miles from the old city of York, dating back to Roman times. It would have been nice to have some time for sight seeing.

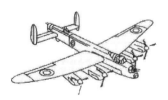

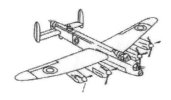

"The Bomber Offensive was the most continuous and the most gruelling operation of war ever carried out. It lasted for some two thousand days and nights and served as the only effective weapon at the throat of Hitler's Germany for four years."

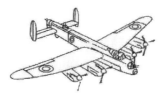

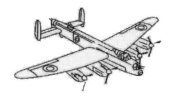

Few people in England could have guessed, in those days, what the eventual cost would be for that sustained offensive.

The Bomber Command War Diaries tell us that of the one hundred twenty-five thousand aircrew who entered the Command, seventy-three thousand seven hundred forty-one became casualties; fractionally under 60% of the total.

The only other wartime military service that had a worse record was the German U-Boat Service. They lost eight out of every ten of their submariners.

But those statistics were still far off in the future on that cold and rainy day when we first arrived at 408 Squadron. Each of us was given a cot and small wooden locker in what used to be the library of an old, stately home some five walking miles from the base. One soon learned not to miss the one morning bus that took you to breakfast and to work.

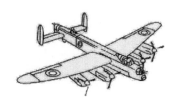

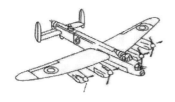

A short walk out of the back door of our 'stately home' away from home brought you to the bank of the Ouse River where a boatman would ferry you across the river to the picture postcard old village of Nun Monkton with its village duck pond, maypole and old pub (The Alice Hawthorn) where you could usually find some eggs and chips and a pint or two of beer.

It would be hard to find a greater contrast than sitting on the grass in this seventeenth century village and watching the newest in war-making technology flying through the skies around the base a few miles away.

My old buddy from Claresholm and Summerside days had gone to different schools, but toward the same bomber squadron goal. Some months later when I had a few days leave I went to see him at Kings Lynn in East Anglia.

He met me at the train and we went out to his mess and about an hour later he was told he was on an operational trip to Berlin that night.

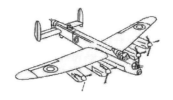

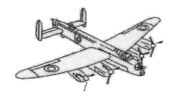

I watched them take off and waited in vain for his return.

It was a terrible train ride back to my own squadron at Linton.

But I am getting ahead of myself.

It was now time for some of my past sins to catch up with me. I was sitting blissfully in the pilot's room one morning when I got a summons to go to the Chief Training Officers office. Puzzled by the call I dutifully trundled off to the office of the great man who is a somewhat ancient Wing Commander with some World War One ribbons and a magnificent great handlebar moustache.

As I enter and salute I see the sparks coming off of this crusty, no-nonsense fellow. He begins by telling me that my personal file has finally caught up with me after its arrival from Canada. And that it tells him that I have been trained in the Specialist Navigator course at the General Reconnaissance School at Summerside.

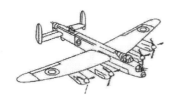

He had also observed that when I arrived at Bournemouth I had given Bomber Command as my first, second and third choices for postings.

The Wing Commander glowered at me for a long moment.

I wondered if he would really take me off this course and this crew, and re-route me to a Coastal Command training station.

He expounded at length about the great costs involved in my government having trained me, in the wisdom of the Personnel Directorate who made the selection for my training path and so on and so on.

I stood rigidly at attention through this long diatribe and then realizing that he had no intention of taking me off of the course I managed not to smile until after I had been dismissed and left his office.

The rest of the pilots in the pilot's room looked at me with a raised eyebrow but since I seemed to have a whole skin they made no comment and I was content to keep them wondering.

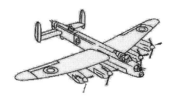

Two days later the Daily Routine Orders (DRO's) announced my promotion to Flight Sergeant and I happily put up the crown over the three stripes on my uniform sleeve.

After a few days I became aware that none of my fellow pilots or none of the crew genuflected when I came in the room. How unflinchingly pedestrian this rabble was.

So I settled back into joyful membership in the human race and lived happily ever after. Most of the time.

We had a few beers as a modest graduation celebration, said a fond farewell to the splendid Wellington and packed out kit bags. In the morning we were taken to the train station and made our way to the old city of York.

We were the only crew destined for 408 Squadron and the Canadian Group, all the other crews went into RAF squadrons.

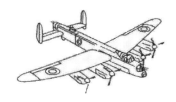

This selection has remained a mystery to me to this day. But it did have one very important consequence for us, and that was that we were going to one of the three squadrons in Bomber Command that were flying the Mark 11 Lancaster.

The Mark 11 Lancaster had four Hercules radial engines, each with 1650 horsepower instead of the other Marks of the Lancaster that had the Rolls Royce Merlin 1200 horsepower engines.

We arrived at the Heavy Conversion Unit (HCU) at Eastmoor and were given a flight engineer and a mid upper gunner to round out our crew.

The HCU had Mark 1 Lancasters and the engineer and I had to get familiar with the gauges and our routines rather quickly. We did the ubiquitous circuits and bumps and soon were given an instructor's approval to go solo. As he climbed out of the plane, it looked as if he was saying a silent prayer of thanks for having been delivered from some dire and threatening fate.

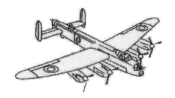

The Chips Are Down

Unlike the American bombers that always carried two pilots, the British bombers only had one.

This meant that when a new pilot arrived at a British bomber squadron there was only one way in that he could get some experience - that was to go as a 'second dickey' with an experienced crew.

The new pilot would simply stand behind the engineer and watch, and listen on the intercom, to the splendid entertainment of the evening that had been prepared for your enjoyment by your German hosts.

The searchlights, the flak, and the night fighters with their streams of tracers looking like pretty lights, all managed to capture your attention and admiration and to keep you somewhat focused, as it were.

After two of these 'second dickey' trips you were ready to take your own crew on their first evening outing to admire the 'son et lumière' entertainment.

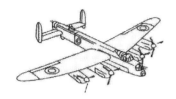

But back to the real world, 408 Squadron at Linton-on-Ouse. Now, with crew in place and my second dickeys behind me, it was time to find my own evening's entertainment in the skies over Germany.

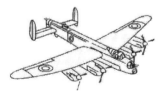

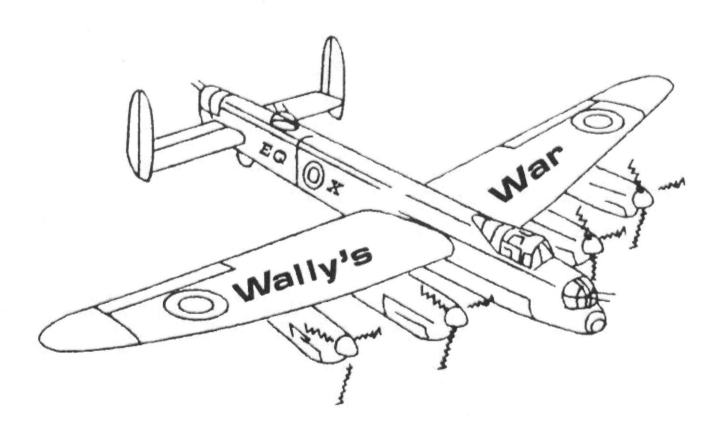

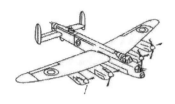

Berlin
20/21 January, 1944

This was my first 'second dickey' trip with Flight Lieutenant Eldon Kearl from Raymond, Alberta. He was one of the senior pilots on the squadron and everything about him and his crew was very impressive.

The quiet functioning of the crew, meshing together like a well-oiled machine, was obvious even to my unpracticed eye.

He would have three more trips to do to complete his tour.

On his last but one he would go missing, later the crew was reported dead.

It came as a shock to everyone on the squadron as he was liked by all, but came as a significant shock to me who could only ask myself if a crew that good and experienced 'bought the farm', as we used to say, what chance, then, for us?

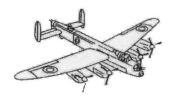

This night over Berlin brought a high-level cloud cover.

The Pathfinder Force (the bomber squadrons who marked the targets for the rest of us to drop our bombs) used their parachute-borne coloured flares so we could approach on a precise heading and then release our bombs.

Seven hundred sixty-nine bombers attacked the target that night.

Thirty-five of these bombers were lost through enemy action.

Because of the heavy cloud cover no reconnaissance aircraft were able to photograph the target for four days.

Seven flying hours for this trip.

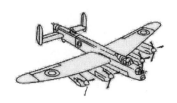

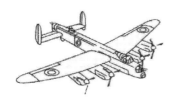

Magdeburg.
21/22 January, 1944

Again I am the guest of Flt. Lt. Kearl. Six hundred forty-eight bombers were sent on this first major raid to this old city. T

The forecast winds were badly skewed and much confusion resulted.

Fifty-seven bombers were lost.

On our return to England we were advised that our bases in Yorkshire were fogged in and we were to land at an American base near Newmarket and stay the night.

Six hours and ten minutes flying time.

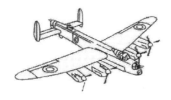

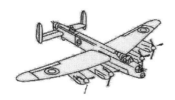

Berlin.
30/31 January, 1944.

First trip with my own crew:

Frank Elbourn - navigator   Royal Air Force
Ross Scott - wireless operator   Royal Canadian Air
Force
Larry Newton - flight engineer   Royal Air Force
Mike Nelligan - bomb aimer   Royal Canadian Air
Force
Andre Blais - mid-upper gunner Royal Canadian Air
Force
Jack Moore - rear gunner   Royal Canadian Air
     Force

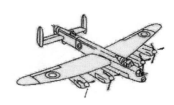

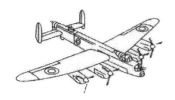

Five hundred thirty-four aircraft attacked the target and thirty-three were lost.

The troops had the full range of German expertise and activity on display, and were rather awed by it all.

For the crew it was a hard look at the real world in that they would live for the next few months.

Seven hours and fifteen minutes flying time.

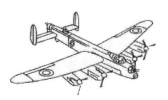

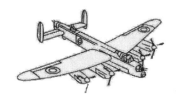

Augsburg.
25/26 February, 1944.

After two weeks of leave we arrive back at base just in time to be one of the five hundred ninety-four chosen crews to visit this old city with its fabulous architectural and artistic heritage.

Augsburg also had aircraft component factories, paper and textile mills, so necessary for the war effort.

It was an unusually cold night, so much so that the nearby River Loire froze over and many of the firefighting water hoses froze, hampering their efforts somewhat.

The raid was an outstanding success causing the German propaganda machine to label it as "terror bombing". Any bombing raid brought terror with it, an essential component, you might say, but then that had been obvious since the early days
at Guernica, Warsaw, Rotterdam,
London or Coventry.

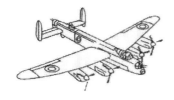

Perhaps the difference was that this was now happening in Germany.

Twenty-five bombers were lost.

Eight hours and five minutes flying time.

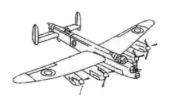

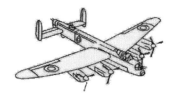

Le Mans, France.
7/8 March, 1944

It has been nine days since the last operational trip, but that does not mean we haven't been busy.

The training schedules are heavy when we are not on "ops" - practice bombing runs on targets laid out on the Yorkshire moors with small smoke bombs, and then we play games with the Spitfire pilots from a nearby unit who pretend to be attacking German fighters while the pilot and gunners practice their evasive action tactics.

The navigators are quite pleased to stay at base while the rest of us are doing this.

As a small aside to illustrate the importance of checking the bombsight and doing the bombing practice, we became famous, or was it infamous, for being the only 408 crew to bomb a British pub because of an improperly calibrated bomb sight.

On our first run of the exercise, we could not see the bomb exploding on the ground.

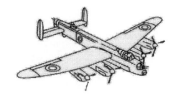

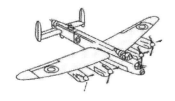

We abandoned the exercise and on arriving back at base were told that the bomb had landed some miles away, in the middle of a small village square that had an old stone church on one side and a pub on the other.

No damage done, but the single old fellow who was waiting outside the pub door for the place to open on this Sunday morning - it was about a quarter to noon- was almost frightened into joining the temperance union.

I would never have guessed, during those 'fighter affiliation' exercises with those Spitfires, that in the not-too-distant-future would be flying one of them and doing the exercises with the bombers.

The training schedule included long cross-country exercises to keep the navigators fine-tuned, as well as hours of 'dinghy drill' in a rather cold pool of water simulating our having to get out of a bomber that has been forced to ditch in the North Sea. But back to Le Mans.

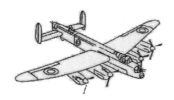

Le Mans was a very important railway junction and siding, especially so now that the Germans were building up the 'West Wall' defences against the invasion that they knew was coming in the not-too-distant future.

These sidings were usually congested with troop trains and goods trains, all waiting to get out to their proper destinations.

The French underground sometimes managed to get information on such a build-up out to the British, and then it was necessary to quickly mount a raid on the location. This time Command assigned three hundred four aircraft on a rather successful surprise raid.

No losses for the raid. My first kindergarten raid.

The very energetic Germans had the place repaired and functioning again by the night of the 13/14 March and they were again honoured by the presence of a bunch of bombers. Fifteen locomotives, eight hundred freight cars, two nearby factories, and a demolished rail siding was the night's take.

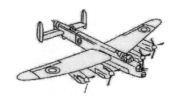

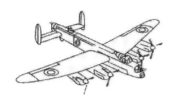

Frankfurt-am-Main
18/19 March, 1944

There are two cities named Frankfurt in Germany; one on the Mainz river and a second one farther east on the Oder . You may be sure we never got them mixed up. Eight hundred forty-six aircraft attacked the city with the Pathfinder Force, again doing their splendid work in getting the target markers down, in place, and on time.

There were diversionary raids to try to draw off some of the night fighters from the route of the main force bomber stream; one on Heliogland and some lovely work at the night fighter bases themselves.

Mosquito long-range night fighters would be at the German bases about the time they estimated the German night fighters would be ready for takeoff, and then as the Germans were heading off down the runway the Mosquitos would shoot them down and shoot up the rest of the base before going home.

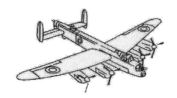

It sounds like a fabulously dirty trick, but it was one the British learned from the Germans and then developed into an art form.

We learned, as a crew, to be very careful with our aircraft riding lights when we got back to England. We knew the sky was full of unseen bombers, but we also saw, on many occasions, a returning bomber being shot down close to an English airfield that had its landing lights on for the returning aircraft. It was a ghastly situation.

The bombers were now getting close to their fuel limits, so they had to land, and the airfield lights had to be on for them to land, so it was an ideal made-to-order opportunity for a German night fighter to prowl around shooting up the bombers and causing the maximum possible damage in the air and on the ground.

We soon learned to keep our aircraft lights off until we were close to base and knew all was well. But, back to Frankfurt.

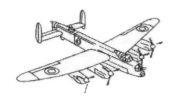

The total aircraft out on the various activities for the night were one thousand forty-six, and the losses were twenty-two bombers.

The trip was not at all sweetness and light for us.

Fortunately, no one was hurt, but it was a near rum thing as the bullets that penetrated the wing had also penetrated the plexiglass between my head and the navigator's stations.

We landed at the first base we could get to in East Anglia, and next day another crew from Linton came and brought us home.

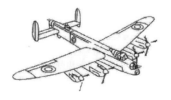

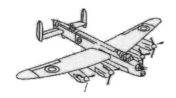

Berlin
24/25 March, 1944

Eight hundred eleven aircraft attacked the target with the loss of seventy-two bombers to the German defences.

It was an 8.9 percent loss. One that no military force could sustain for very long; men and machines could not be replaced at that rate.

It would be the last major raid on Berlin and the end of what has been called "The Battle of Berlin". There would continue to be the small nuisance raids on the city - small groups of high-flying Mosquito bombers; just enough to alert the air raid sirens and get the people out of bed and into the bomb shelters, night after night after night.

This raid was known as the 'night of the strong winds'. We had left England heading nearly straight east to Flensburg and then set course southeast to Berlin.

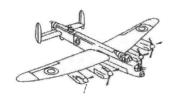

In those days we knew nothing about jet streams, but that is what we had and almost dead astern; a wind we later calculated at 120 miles an hour.

We were given a wind speed of about half that by the meteorologists, and our clever navigator had increased his estimate to nearly 90, but still we were ahead of where we should be on our approach to the target.

Our speed along the ground was airspeed 265 plus the wind speed one hundred twenty for a total of three hundred eighty-five.

Fabulous, but nearly fatal.

We could not bomb until the Pathfinder markers had gone down, and as we approached the target area we could see that the defences were in high gear. A clear sky gave the searchlights full scope, and there was a huge belt of flak guns placed around the city.

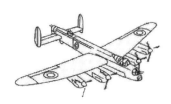

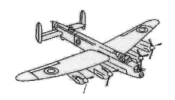

As we were driving through the middle of this large area looking anxiously for the marker flares so we could drop our bombs, we got to the southern rim when the rear gunner announced that the marker flares had just gone down behind us.

As I turned sharply to the left to go around so we could get a decent bombing run on the flares, unbeknownst to me we were heading right into that stiff wind, and our speed had just gone from 385 to 145 - we were almost standing still.

At that moment the radar had us and about 50 searchlights had us cornered - hard to count with that blaze of light blinding you. Controlled by the radar was the flak - hundreds of guns concentrating on us.

To add to the confusion, the patrolling night fighters were making themselves felt. We still had our bomb load on board, plus a bit more than half our fuel load.

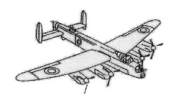

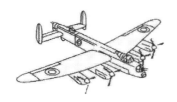

We came heading in at just over twenty thousand feet, and after the evasive action was over, and we had escaped from the searchlights, flak, and fighters, we were at about eight thousand feet.

How the aircraft held together during that violent, evasive action I'll never know.

As we stabilized the aircraft, and the crew sorted themselves out from where they had been flung about. We turned back to the scene of the action and began a slow climb back to where we could release our bombs and get on a heading for home.

It was not a very inviting task to try and go through that target area at that height with all those hundreds of bombers above you, but we went through, and then the navigator gave us a heading for the route home.

At this altitude we would be without the protection of the mass of the bombers, and vulnerable to the radar. We would also be using fuel we could ill afford since it always takes more fuel to climb. But the gremlins were not yet done with us.

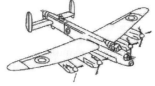

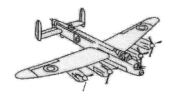

As we got to about seventeen thousand feet on track between Osnabruck and Munster, gradually falling farther and farther behind the main force of the bombers, one of the few flak guns they had there got lucky, and a piece of shrapnel cut a hole about a foot or so in diameter out of the exhaust pipe in the port inner engine.

There I was flying along in the night sky with a huge candle of flame shooting out of the engine about eight feet from where I was sitting.

The engine was working perfectly well, but in the night skies of Germany in those days, no one needed advertising of this kind.

We feathered the engine and now had a new problem. It always takes more fuel to fly on three engines than on four, and we were already getting to the margins on fuel. We were all alone in the night sky above Germany, getting farther and farther away from the main stream of the bomber force that was our best protection from the radar.

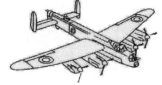

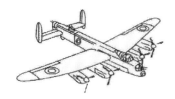

It seemed a bit lonely, but the gunners got their adrenalin flowing and we went on our way towards the North Sea and home.

When we could see the Dutch coastline in the early morning light, it was obvious how vulnerable we were to any German fighter in that sky, so I asked the wireless operator to break silence and ask for a Spitfire escort to meet us and escort us to the emergency landing aerodrome at Woodbridge.

Few sights could be as welcome as the early morning light reflecting off of the wings of that squadron of Spitfires as they rose in the sky like a flock of chicks around a mother hen.

They buzzed around us as we approached the English coast and waved to us as they went back to their base.

Again we left our aircraft to be repaired and got a ride home next day with one of our planes from Linton.

All in all, a night to be remembered, but hopefully, never to be repeated.

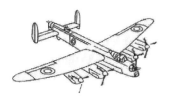

Seven hours and thirty-five minutes flying time.

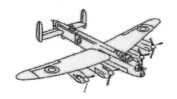

Essen
26/27 March, 1944

Seven hundred and five bombers went back to the heavily defended Ruhr Valley industrial area after having been away for some time dealing with targets that were deep inside Germany.

Only nine aircraft were lost so the Germans must have been taken by surprise and had their night fighters staged on beacons that were located deeper in the eastern regions.

Their radar was very good, but with the large bomber mass of aircraft they could only pick up a general direction and height.

The German night fighters would have to get into the stream of bombers and pick up such targets as they could. They would work in teams of three or four with each of them carrying a number of high intensity flares that they could drop in turn; magnesium flares that would momentarily blind the pilot and gunners of the bombers.

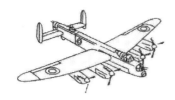

The German night fighters would have teammates, coming behind them, who could spot bombers in the flare light and they would try to shoot one down on each pass. They wore special night glasses to keep them from being blinded by the light of the flares.

Very good tactics and very successful. It was a very quiet trip for us.

Five hours and twenty minutes flying time.

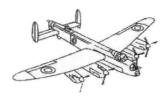

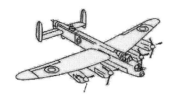

Nürnberg
30/31 March, 1944

Seven hundred and ninety-five bombers were sent out and ninety five were lost to the enemy defences, mainly the night fighters.

This was the worst single night loss of the war, 11.9 percent and coming on top of the recent 72 lost on the evening of the 24/25 March on Berlin.

It sent shock waves throughout Britain and Bomber Command.

This raid was the first time that Bomber Command had operated during the full moon period. At our altitude, on a clear night during the full moon period, there was enough light to easily see another bomber in the sky, so darkness was a cherished ally.

However, the powers that be made their decision and away we went.

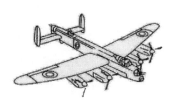

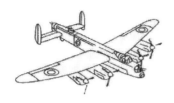

The route selected took us between two unknown beacons around that the night fighters orbited awaiting the arrival of their potential targets.

It was just sheer bad luck for us and must have been like shooting fish in a barrel for the Germans.

Perhaps I should pause here for a moment and note that when the ammunition belts were put together for the guns (ours and theirs) every tenth bullet would have a phosphorous coating so it would be visible. As the stream of bullets came out of a gun, they would look like a continuous coloured line coming from an unseen source. Very pretty in the sky, but to be avoided like the plague.

During much of the trip there was a great deal of enemy activity visible to us, that just kept the adrenalin flowing, but for us it was one of the quietest trips we had ever done. No one came near us.

There was a good deal of concern back at base and at all levels.

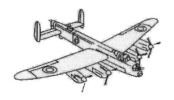

Many people were assessing this situation, and we were asking ourselves if the Germans had some new weapon that had taken this massive toll of 167 bombers in the past week.

There were no indicators of anything new in the German skies - Berlin and Nürnberg were just unlucky accidents.

Each squadron could only fly a maximum of 18 aircraft on any one night, so this week's loss was roughly equivalent to nine squadrons.

At Lissett, a 4 Group base not far from us, they sent out 18 Halifax bombers and one returned.

The crew was posted away and the squadron closed.

Each afternoon at 1:00 pm the British Broadcasting Corporation would start off their newscast with the announcer saying, "Aircraft of Bomber Command attacked _____ last night. _____ of our aircraft are missing." and then go with details and other news items.

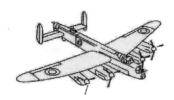

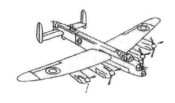

We would by then have finished our lunch and everyone in the mess would be very quiet. It would be our first awareness of the total losses for the previous evening.

Each crew lost represented at least seven men, and the announcement of the 95 lost on the Nürnberg raid brought a stunned silence to the mess.

The Allied invasion of Europe was only ten weeks away, so the focus of Bomber Command activity shifted away from the targets deep in Germany to the military buildup along the coast of Europe - the defences the Germans called the 'West Wall'.

The Germans had been working overtime to bring their guided missiles into service and were building bases for launching them onto their English targets. They were nasty, demoralizing, and did a lot of damage. Most of these targets were well hidden in France, and being quite small, they presented accuracy problems for the Pathfinders and for us.

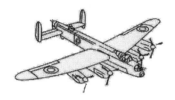

Perhaps we should pause here for a moment and shed some light on the Pathfinder Force we've referred to a few times.

These were a few squadrons of experienced bomber crews, given special navigation equipment, who would send a few of their aircraft under the control of a "Master Bomber".

We all listened on a special radio frequency for any instructions they might wish to give in relation to the target.

The Pathfinders would get to the target, identify it, and then at a specified time, drop a coloured flare on the target for the rest of us in Main Force, to drop our bombs on. The colours would change every raid.

When the target was covered by clouds, the Pathfinders dropped large parachute-borne flares, and we would then drop our bombs on a precise heading using those flares as markers.

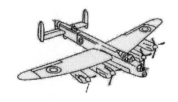

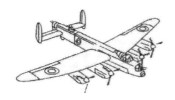

It was less precise than ground marking and more hazardous for the bombers, as the enemy fighters knew we would have to approach on a precise heading.

The Pathfinder crews had to be very precise in their timing and in their target identification. It meant that they had to get down to low levels to do this, making them very vulnerable to the enemy defences.

When one of their marker flares burned out they had to lay another that meant they had to stick around the target area until the raid was over.

It was an occupation not known for its longevity.

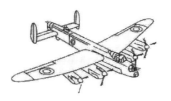

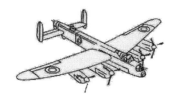

Düsseldorf

22/23 April, 1944

Five hundred and ninety six bomber aircraft were sent out to this centre of heavy industry, iron and steel, in the Ruhr Valley. Twenty nine aircraft were lost. It was a very quiet trip for us.

Five hours and twenty minutes flying time.

When the BBC news announcement told us that "29 aircraft were missing" after the Dusseldorf raid, I remember being a bit perplexed at the reaction of my messmates. Earlier, when the announcement of the seventy-two losses on Berlin, and the ninety-five losses on Nürnberg was made there was a discernible reaction of shock. Now, we seemed to accept this level of loss.

I thought about the 29 crew, 29 x 7 equals a minimum of 203 men - perhaps more with second dickeys and special radar operators.

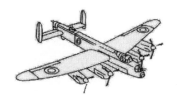

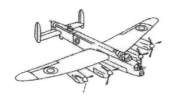

What does 203 men represent in terms of mothers and fathers, sisters and brothers, wives and children, not to mention the aunts and uncles and grandmothers and grandfathers?

We would not know until after the war was over and the numbers were crunched up that the total Bomber Command aircrew losses were more than 73 thousand. Imagine that in terms of families - British, Canadian, Australian, New Zealand, South African, United States.

Perhaps this would be a good place to digress for a moment and let you look at what a day in the life of a squadron pilot would look like.

Up and shower and shave in time to get the bus to the mess for breakfast, and then each of us would go to their sections.

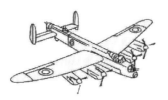

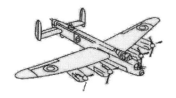

Each aircrew trade had their own section where they would be briefed by the section head as to the day's activities; new specialist information and so on. Then the pilot, flight engineer, and the wireless operator would go out to their aircraft dispersal to do the serviceability check on the aircraft, and, if necessary, take the plane up for an air check.

If we were going to be on 'ops' that night, the ground crew would be loading the bombs and fuel.

We then went to lunch, and if we were 'on' we might go back to the quarters and get a few hours sleep before we had our evening meal and went to the briefing room for the outline of the night's work.

The briefing was always the last thing we did before we took off so we would have our flying gear on and, as soon as the briefing was over, we caught a bus out to the dispersal.

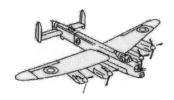

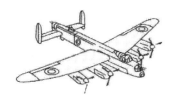

At the briefing we had the route outlined on a large wall map and each of the specialists, intelligence, meteorology, and so on, would outline their current information. Then we got into the bus and went off to dispersal to get ready to go.

Each aircraft taxied out to the 'take off' position, and when we were given the green light, we turned onto the runway and opened up the throttles and started to roll. With take off speed we lifted off and were gone into the night on our first heading, climbing to altitude to go across the North Sea and to the reception the Germans had planned for us.

The Germans were very competent, technically as well as operationally. They divided their geographic regions into large areas or 'boxes' in that the radar, flak, and fighters were staged. The fighters gathered at various heights around beacons so they could be controlled by the ops managers on the ground who determined the direction and height of the stream of approaching bombers.

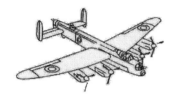

The bombers in the main stream threw 'window' out of each aircraft.

'Window' was thousands of strips of aluminum foil, each piece some 8 or 10 inches long and about a third or half an inch in width.

As this mass of strips came out of each aircraft, it gave a great reflection to the radar below, and made it impossible for them to identify any particular aircraft in the stream. Hence our greatest safety lay in being in the mass of the main stream of the bombers.

When, for any reason, you found yourself out of the protective cover of this main stream, you became very vulnerable as the radar could pinpoint you for the flak guns, the searchlights, and the night fighters.

If two fighters had you in sight and worked together, your survival chances were diminished somewhat.

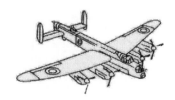

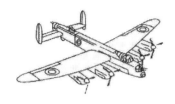

Perhaps we could consider another small piece of equipment we carried at this point. It was a backward looking radar that scanned the sky vertically and horizontally behind the bomber.

It was only in the Lancaster 11 (only 200 copies were built and only three squadrons flew them until they ran out and were replaced with Halifaxes and other marks of the Lancaster) that they were installed, presumably as experimental models.

The wireless operator would look at the small screen he had and when he saw a blip that was moving faster than the many blips that were reflections from the bombers nearby, he would alert the gunners.

We tended to regard the thing, its code name was 'Monica', as more of a nuisance than a help. We were by no means conscientious in using it. I recall being told by other pilots that they didn't use it at all.

They thought it distracted the gunners from keeping a wider surveillance field.

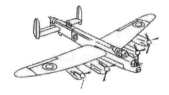

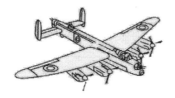

About a month after I had left the squadron I went one rainy day to the small intelligence room we had on that base and found a recent intelligence bulletin describing how the invasion forces had captured a German airfield with an intact Jerkers 88 night fighter.

On the console of the fighter was the legend (in German, of course) "Device for homing on Monica".

Obviously the clever Germans had captured a Mark 11 Lancaster shortly after they were brought into service, and assuming that all bombers would be equipped with Monica, they developed a counter measure very quickly.

Our erstwhile jokes about "Monica, our lady of the evening who was not to be trusted" turned out to be less of a joke than we had thought.

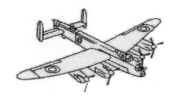

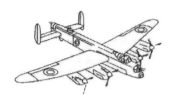

Düsseldorf
22/23 April, 1944

Five hundred ninety-six bombers were sent to this heavy industry centre in the heart of the Ruhr Valley (sometimes known as 'Happy Valley' by the working troops).

The Ruhr Valley targets had not been given much attention while the "Battle of Berlin" was in high gear from November to mid March.

No doubt they had missed us as they seemed to have everything in readiness to insure a warm welcome for our return.

Twenty-nine aircraft were lost, but there was widespread damage in the industrial areas.

For us, it was a very quiet trip.

Five hours and twenty minutes flying time for the night's work.

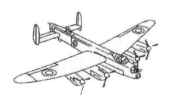

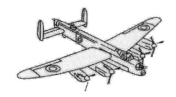

On our return to base after a trip, we would call in for landing clearance and be given our number based on the other aircraft that were ahead of us.

After landing, a small truck would pick us up at the dispersal and take us to the debriefing where the intelligence experts would get all the information on the trip, and anything we had seen that was new or newsworthy.

It would then be time for our bacon and eggs breakfast, and then we'd go off to bed for a few hours sleep.

Every three months we would get two weeks leave, with a free railway pass to wherever we wanted to go in Britain.

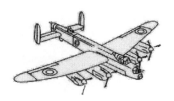

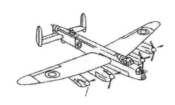

Essen
26/27 April, 1944

Four hundred ninety-three bombers were assigned to visit Essen again. Essen was one of the heavy iron and steel centres - forgings and castings for vehicles, tanks, guns, and other such equipment. The Pathfinders were at their usual best, and the raid was a successful one.

The raid was not without interest for us as a night fighter picked us up and gave us a 'squirt' just as we were moving out of his way. These fellows had 50 calibre guns that gave them a range superior to our 303 calibre guns, and a considerable advantage.

If they had the range proper and their guns were on target, their bullet pattern could hardly be anything but lethal for a bomber, but we were lucky again and were moving away as he opened fire. We got a bunch of bullets through the plane, but no crew member or vital aircraft system was damaged.

Five hours and five minutes flying time.

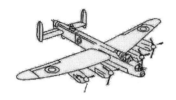

Friedrichshafen
27/28 April, 1944

Three hundred twenty-two Lancasters went to this target located on the German side of Lake Constance, with Switzerland on the other.

The target was a series of factories that made gear boxes and engines for tanks.

We were a bit apprehensive as this was again in the full moon period, and Nurnburg was only four weeks behind us. However, the Pathfinders were at their best again, and this made the attack a success.

Later reconnaissance showed this to be the worst damage the engine factories had suffered during the war.

The Lancs made it to the target without the night fighters intercepting them, but the return trip was another story.

Eighteen were lost.

There was the story at the time, perhaps apocryphal, of the bomber that had strayed across the lake into Swiss territory.

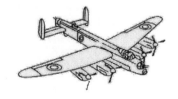

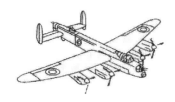

The flak came up on the Swiss side and the Swiss called the bomber to advise them that they had strayed above Swiss territory. The pilot replied, "Yes, we know." and then told them that "the flak is a few thousand feet below". To this the Swiss replied, "Yes, we know".

Total flying time was nine hours and five minutes.

It was a very interesting trip with the lake and the mountains clearly visible in the moonlight. It was a pity that we could not spend more time admiring the scene below, but the Germans had managed to make us feel unwelcome so we turned for home. My further acquaintance with the city would have to wait until years later when I was stationed at Four Wing in Germany.

Just as an aside, Friedrichshafen was the city in that the airships, or Zeppelins of the First World War and subsequently, were made, and sent on their way until the final explosion in the United States brought the airship activity to its end.

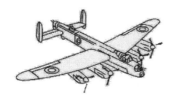

Ghent
10/11 may 1944

Five hundred six bombers were sent to deal with the railway siding/marshalling yards at Courtrai, Dieppe, Ghent, Lens and Lille in Belgium and France.

One hundred twenty-three bombers were sent to attack another of the large railway junction/marshaling yards that were servicing the 'West Wall' preparations in Europe.

We were told to be extra careful with our bombing run, as these Belgians were our allies.

As usual, the Pathfinders were very good and the raid went well, with minimal damage beyond the marshalling yards themselves.

Three hours and fifty minutes flying time.

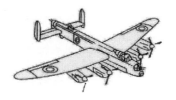

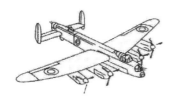

Dortmund
4/5 May,1944

This target had not seen any Bomber Command activity for a year. Three hundred seventy-five aircraft were assigned to attack the city, and eighteen of these were lost. This is a 4.8 percent loss, but for 408 Squadron it was a truly sad occasion.

Our squadron commander, Wing Commander Dave Jacobs from Waterloo, Ontario, had done his first tour of operations on 408 on Hampden bombers.

Later he had picked up the members of his first crew and come back for a second tour. His crew members were all section leaders in their respective trades. They would have two more trips to do after this one on Dortmund, to finish their second tour.

One of the other squadron pilots, who was a few hundred feet above and behind saw them quite clearly as they were silhouetted against the searchlights shining on the clouds a few thousand feed below the bomber stream.

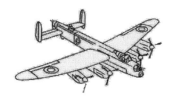

As they were approaching the target for their bombing run, a flak burst hit them in the bomb bay, and the aircraft blew up with a blast that shook up the aircraft nearby.

The squadron, and all its sections, was left leaderless, and everyone there was in a state of shock.

It is hard to imagine a finer leader and a more accomplished pilot than Dave Jacobs. About a week after I had checked into the squadron, I was out at a dispersal doing an ordinary check on an aircraft before we went on an exercise.

I was sitting in the pilot's seat with the window open as the Wing Commander's little truck came to a stop by the aircraft. He couldn't have known I was there, and as he got out of the truck he came over to one of the ground crew chaps and asked him about his child who had had the mumps.

Since there were several hundred of the ground crew chaps on the squadron, knowing all about them and their families was no mean accomplishment.

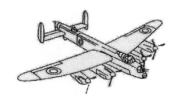

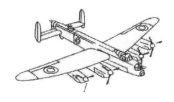

He would, of course, also know all his aircrew in the same way. His loss was an unmitigated tragedy for 408 Squadron. His like was not to be seen again.

However, we were not aware of this while we were approaching Dortmund, and we soon had some modest problems of our own.

As we ended our bombing run and the Bomb Aimer said 'bombs away', we did a sharp turn to the right and closed the bomb bay doors. It was then that a German night fighter started to shoot at us, just as the gunner gave me the command to vacate the space we were in.

This command always took priority over anything else I can think of, so the aircraft went into a violent turn and climb that was less than welcome to the navigator and the wireless operator.

They were sitting in their little cubicles enclosed by a curtain that hid the light they needed to do their work from the rest of the world.

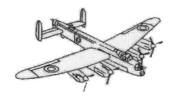

As the aircraft went into a violent climbing turn, they and the instruments of their magical trades were scattered to the four corners of the aircraft.

We never learned to overcome the law of gravity, and they usually were a bit sore and battered about by these games the pilot and gunners would play.

Sometimes they understood that this was the lesser of two evils, but they nevertheless grumped mightily.

War is hell, as we used to say to them when they showed us their bruises.

In any case, I digress again. I should mention that we were carrying a second dickey that night, one Pilot Officer Burnell. When we started to move with the fighter's attack he, the engineer, the navigator, the wireless operator, and the bomb aimer in the nose, all obeyed the time-honoured demands of the laws of gravity, and found themselves on
the floor of the aircraft.

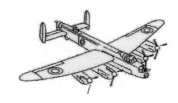

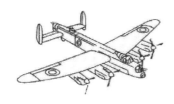

Our routine was, that when the aircraft was again stabilized, to have each member of the crew check in on the intercom so we could assess the damage and then take necessary action.

Each crew member checked in as being OK, so we went back to our required course and let the engineer check for any damage the bullets had done to the aircraft.   As Larry, the engineer, was doing his fuel and systems check, we heard a thump over the intercom and another crew check brought no answer from the wireless operator.   The navigator was asked to check on Scotty, the W/Op and soon reported back that he was laying on the floor, unconscious, in a pool of blood.

We had a small fold-down cot on one side wall of the aircraft, so the engineer and the navigator got Scotty on it and tried to bandage him up and stop the bleeding.   R e g r e t t a b l y, someone had stolen the morphine out of the first aid kit, but they bandaged him up and got back to the business at hand - getting back to Jolly Olde England.

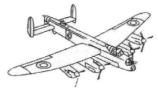

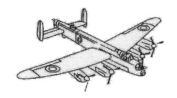

A little farther on the mid upper gunner told us that he too had been hit by an explosive cannon shell shrapnel, but said it wasn't too bad and he would stay in his turret since we still had some distance to go back to base.

We got him out of the turret and bandaged as best they could (we found out later that a bunch of small pieces of this shrapnel had hit him in the chest and face, by a miracle not hitting one of his eyes).

The shortest route to a hospital was at the emergency landing aerodrome at Woodbridge. We called for landing clearance, and they had an ambulance standing by as we came in, and it took the lot of us to the hospital.

They had a crusty old English medical officer there who took Scotty and Andre into his surgery, giving the rest of us each a four ounce bottle of Pusser's navy rum, and he stood there while we all forced it down in one gulp.

In two minutes we were in bed in another wing. We slept until next morning.

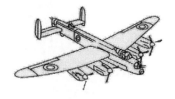

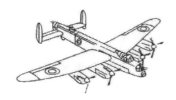

We never saw Scotty again. In a few days he was back in Canada, and in a few months was invalided out of the air force.

Andre came back to the squadron in a couple of months and on his first trip with another crew, was shot down over Hamburg.

Again we left our aircraft at Woodbridge to be repaired and got a ride back to Linton with one of our squadron colleagues. Since we had no aircraft and needed to patch up the crew, we were sent on a week's leave to gather ourselves together.

The evening of my return to Linton I met with Jack Moore, the rear gunner (who had been Scotty's best buddy) and he told me that he did not want to fly again. He felt that he had let the crew down in not preventing that night fighter attack, and thought he would not be able to do his job properly any more.

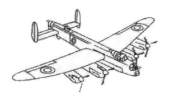

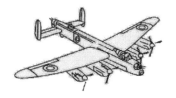

I was somewhat taken aback, and after some discussion suggested that I had every confidence in him and would he sleep on it.

If he was convinced that he was no longer confident in his ability to do the job, he and I could go to see the squadron commander in the morning and discuss the matter.

In the morning his mind was unchanged, so I could not, and felt I should not, try to change his mind and try to force him to continue on.

The consequences of his decision were not going to be pleasant and he knew this, but I felt that this was his decision to make and not mine, and that I should not try to unduly influence him.

We went to see the Wing Commander who listened to Jack and them dismissed him rather curtly.

He then proceeded to chew me out in spades for "not being able to keep my crew under control", and then in the rudest possible way, dismissed me.

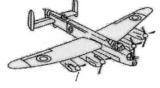

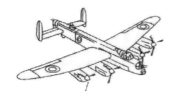

Obviously his value system and mine were not in sync. Even now I am unable to understand the line of logic this new wing commander of ours followed in making his judgment of Jack and me.

This refusal to fly was know in the air force as LMF, or lack of moral fibre, or, as the British Army would phrase it, "cowardice in the face of the enemy".

I would tend to describe this as the air force equivalent of shell shock, and would give the man a chance to gather himself together and reflect at length on the matter.

It was not as if there was a crashing great shortage of gunners, and the world was going to stop turning if Jack didn't fly again.

They had no trouble giving us two new gunners and a wireless op so we could get off onto ops again without impoverishing the human resources of Bomber Command.

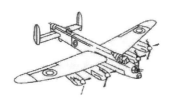

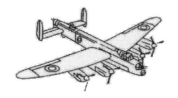

Our new wing commander had his own bee in his bonnet, and he and I would meet again.

There was another sad sequel to the Dortmund night's action.

Our second dickey, Pilot Officer Burnell, took his own crew on the next trip the squadron was on; they were badly shot up with two of his crew killed. He refused to fly again and the wing commander had him arrested and confined to quarters pending court martial. A few days later he committed suicide.

Of course it came as a shock to all of us, but we, as a community had our own superstitions and beliefs. One of these emerged for us at this time. There were always more crews than aircraft available (we could only fly a maximum of eighteen aircraft on any one night) so when you first arrived on the squadron you had to build up a bit of seniority before you were assigned your own aircraft.

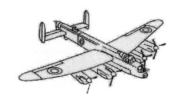

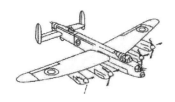

When the flight commander offered me X-ray, I thought it was a bit strange, because there were other crews senior to me who should have been given their own plane, but, without discussion accepted it. I didn't find out until much later that X-ray was considered to be a 'Jonah" as no crew had ever, in the history of the squadron, finished a tour on it.

I remember being amused when I heard this for I assumed that the serviceability and the flying characteristics of X-ray were much the same as the other aircraft on the squadron, and could not figure out how Adolf Hitler had put a hex on the X-ray. On further reflection, it seems that the ground crew had also bought into this superstition. They would, of course, be familiar with the squadron history of X-ray aircraft.

As soon as we took over the 'ownership' of X-ray, the aircrew agreed that they would invite the ground crew over to the Alice Hawthorn pub in Nun Monkton every second week for an 'eggs and chips' dinner and a few pints of beer.

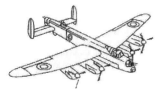

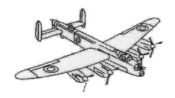

It was a wonderful opportunity for us airmen to get to know the ground crew.

We soon discovered that they had as firm a commitment to X-ray as we did.

Their commitment became more obvious as time went on and we became the only crew, in our time on the squadron, to not ever have a non-starter or an early return from a trip because of a serviceability problem.

These guys did their job and they did it well. We knew that our lives depended on a good -functioning aircraft, and they always gave us one we could depend on.

They had to work outside in the cold, snow, rain, or hot sun, the worst possible conditions, and yet they always did their job to perfection.

They were truly the unsung heroes of the war.

We found out, in talking to them later, that they knew about the superstition of no one ever having finished a tour in X-ray, and that they were keeping their fingers crossed for us.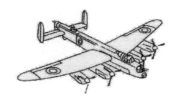

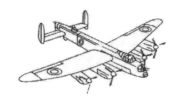

Coutances, France
6/7 June, 1944

Bomber Command had been acting like a tactical Air Force in the days prior to the invasion.

The small targets - railway yards, roads, and bridges essential for German troop movements, an attack on a German army regiment moving into place - in general they softened up the areas the invasion forces would move into in the days to come.

Coutances was an important communications centre in France servicing the railway movement to support the West Wall defences.

There were multiple targets like this in the western European regions, and this evening there were eleven hundred sixty bomber aircraft on a wide variety of targets in this theatre.

Eleven aircraft were lost on the night's operations.

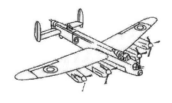

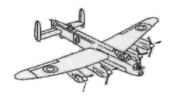

This was the night that the invasion forces crossed the channel and, as we proceeded home from our visit to Coutances the early morning light gave us a spectacular view of the armada of ships on their way to the invasion beaches.

I suspected that my brother, who was in the Canadian Army at Guildford, might be in that mass of ships below. Little did I know that he would be killed a couple of months later at Neufchateau in France.

Eleven aircraft were lost on the night's operations.

Five hours and forty minutes flying time.

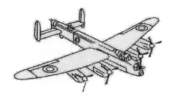

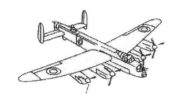

Cambrai
12/13 June, 1944

Cambrai was one of the major marshalling yards in the greater region. The French underground had just provided information to the British that there were ten thousand German troops in railway cars sitting in the yards waiting to be moved to their new defensive positions against the invasion forces.

Speed was of the essence and six hundred bombers, in three groups of two hundred each, were assigned. The first group went over the coast of France at tree top level and then climbed to five hundred feet and bombed from that height.

All bombers were carrying 500-pound anti-personnel bombs. The second group followed two minutes later, and bombed from six hundred feet. The third group went in from seven hundred feet.

We were in the second group and could feel the bomb bursts from the first group. The area was alive with the most intense low level flak we had ever seen.

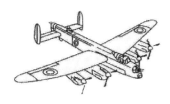

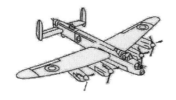

As soon as our bombs were gone we descended to about fifty feet and got on our heading for home, being very watchful for church spires.

We lost three of aircraft from our flight that night, with a curious twist to the story.

Some of the bombers were carrying a mid-under gunner that night. There was a hole in the bottom of the floor of the Lancaster, about the size of a manhole cover and the metal plate that was usually in place could be taken out and a gunner could be strapped in with a rotating set of machine guns on a ring around the hole.

One of the new young gunners on his first trip was sitting in this place looking down for any signs of enemy fighters when their plane was hit and he went out the hole and immediately pulled his parachute rip cord. It opened, and in another second he hit the ground - hard, but was still mobile.

He got out of the harness and headed out of the area as fast as he could go.

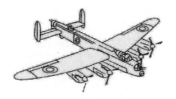

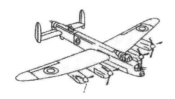

He was French Canadian, and shortly after he was picked up by the French underground, who interrogated him to make sure he was genuine, and then a week later they had him back in England.

Four hours and twenty minutes flying time for the trip.

The total bomber activity for the night on a number of communications facilities in northern Europe was one thousand eighty-three sorties with the loss of forty aircraft. The invasion forces were certainly getting the fullest possible support from Bomber Command.

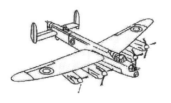

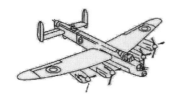

St. Pol
14/15 June, 1944

Three hundred thirty aircraft were again out attacking the railway centres to prevent the German logistic build-up in support of the German armies.

The bombing was hampered by the cloud cover and was less successful than Command had hoped.

Seven hundred sixty-nine bombers were out on all targets, and of these four aircraft were lost.

Three hours and forty-five minutes flying time.

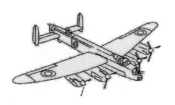

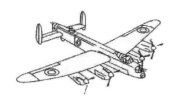

Sterkrade/Holten
16/17 June, 1944

Bomber Command was again out in strength with eight hundred twenty-nine aircraft on a variety of targets, many of them going for the first time, to attack the flying 'buzz bomb' sites.

Three hundred twenty-one went to attack the synthetic fuel plant at Sterkrade/Holten.

The weather forecast was not promising, and there was thick cloud over the target area.

The bombers could only bomb on the airborne markers that the Pathfinders dropped, but that soon disappeared in the heavy cloud.

The raid was not very successful, but the night fighters were active and thirty-two aircraft were lost. All the Germans were fighting to defend their homeland approaches and their authorities had everything available in the air.

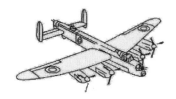

It was a night of furious activity for us as we were attacked on the way to the target, and on the way home.

We had some aircraft damage, but managed to get into the emergency landing aerodrome at Woodbridge and the next day back to base.

We had now been into Woodbridge so often that the other pilots were making jokes about my having a girlfriend down there.

Three hours and twenty minutes flying time.

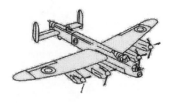

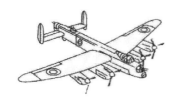

St. Martin-l'Hortier
21 June, 1944

This was our first daylight trip and an opportunity to look at bombing through the eyes of the Americans who did all their work during the daytime. The ones we talked to on the two occasions we were diverted to their bases thought we were absolutely mad to be in the air in those numbers at night.

At night a flak burst is just a small bright red light that flashes, and then is gone. You just want to quickly note how far above or below you it is, and how close to you it is. You are aware that each burst has a lethal radius so you can quickly change your position and/or your altitude and try to avoid the pesky things. They never did seem to be our highest priority items.

However, when we did this first daylight trip and the flak barrage started to come up, we saw for the first time the large, black smoke puff that each burst left, and in a few moments it looked like we were motoring along on a huge blanket of these black puffs.

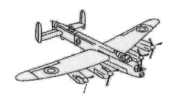

I've never been so scared in all my life. It took a few moments to get in focus on the fact that if you could see the puffs, they were harmless and there was no need to worry; just change position and altitude as need be and you were OK. But the first impression was a massive one.

The target was a buzz bomb site. These things were becoming a problem in London, and doing considerable damage. They were pilotless aircraft with a primitive directional control system and enough fuel on board to take them to London. When they arrived at the end of their fuel, the engine just shut off, and the thing plunged to the ground and produced a huge explosion.

The British quickly developed some fighter squadrons to deal with them as best they could.

An airborne patrolling fighter could quickly catch them up because of their slow speed, and then shoot them out of the sky.

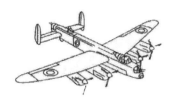

It left a hazardous bunch of bits and pieces in the sky for the attacking pilot to fly through. At night they were quite visible to the attacking fighter because of their long engine exhaust flame, but he always had to expect some damage to his aircraft.

The ground installations for the pilotless aircraft were a bunch of large concrete pads with their attendant machinery for launching the bombs, plus the ancillary shed and tanks for fuel, staff, and of course, the railway tracks.

Not a large target for high-level bombing, and, of course, these things were always located in France or Belgium, so we had to be as precise as we could in the target marking and in our bombing on these targets.

So it was low-level bombing from a few thousand feet, and of course the added attraction was that low-level flak is much more intense
and lethal.

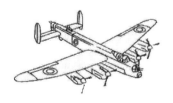

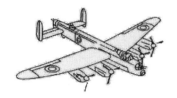

The Germans were counting on this 'special' weapon to help them win the war, and they put all of their available defending fighters into the sky to protect these installations.

Three hundred twenty-two bombers were assigned to three of these targets, but only St. Martin was bombed because of low-level cloud cover on the other two targets.

Five aircraft were lost.

Four hours flying time for the raid.

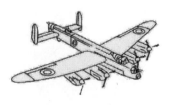

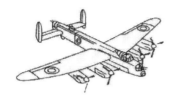

Bentiques
23/24 June , 1944

This was another of the buzz-bomb sites that the Germans had built in northern France. Four hundred twelve aircraft attacked four of these sites this evening.

Five aircraft were lost.

Three hours and forty minutes flying time for the raid.

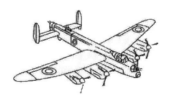

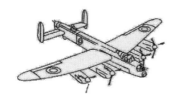

Bamiers
24/25 June, 1944

Another of the buzz-bomb sites that are doing such terrible damage in London.

It is a rainy, stormy night with such high winds that it forces us to use the short runway for takeoff - the first time we have used it.

We have a full bomb load and gas load; and make our way to the end of the runway to take our turn at takeoff.

We get a green light from the controller and turn onto the runway and open the throttles on the brakes and then start to roll.

Temperatures and pressures are normal and our speed builds up. As we are approaching our lift-off speed, but not yet there, we hear a sound like a gunshot and Larry and I know we have blown a tire; just about the worst nightmare a
pilot can imagine.

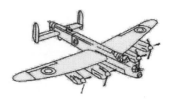

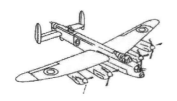

The runway is always kept immaculate by the sweepers to prevent just this sort of thing, but the wind storm has blown a twig or a small stone onto the runway, and with the load we had on board the tire pressure was at maximum.

When some sharp object penetrated the casing, we heard the sound.

Imagine the bad luck that places some small object in our tire's pathway on a surface as large as a runway. The gremlins are really out in force tonight !

Larry, like the superlative engineer he is, recognizes the sound and the danger in the situation. He knows that if we cannot build our speed up to lift-off speed, we will all be splattered across the aerodrome with consequences that are better left unimagined.

It is imperative that we get rid of the undercarriage drag, so, in the wink of an eye, Larry has the undercarriage selector up.

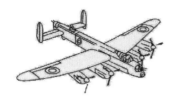

Usually he waits until he gets a signal from me to make the selection, but, thank God, not this time, or we should surely have 'bought the farm'.

The aircraft starts to sink slowly as I try to build up our speed to get into a flying configuration and get up into the sky.

We sink a few feet and then stabilize, and start to climb away. At the end of this short runway is the radio beacon that has some cedar palings about ten feet high around it to protect it from any intrusion by animals or such.

As the doors around the wheel wells close, we hit these palings and do some damage to the starboard wheel well door, but it doesn't interfere with our flying and we climb away into the night sky bound for the target.

If it had not been for Larry's instant recognition of the situation, and his instant action, we would surely have been another statistic.

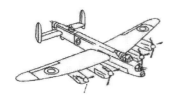

I'm not sure whether any of the other crew members knew what had happened or how close they had been to meeting their maker. If I might borrow a phrase from the Duke of Wellington, "It was a close run thing".

If ever there was an engineer who deserved thanks and commendations for his knowledge and skill it was Larry.

Instead, the wing commander gave me hell for damaging the palings around the beacon. Imagine.

He was within inches of losing an aircraft loaded with gasoline and bombs, a crew, and God only knows what damage might have occurred to the aerodrome had we blown up. His response was to give me a nasty piece of conversation about damaging the palings around the beacon.

I couldn't believe it either, but he did it.

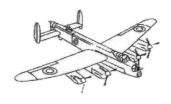

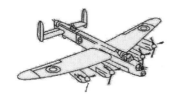

This was not a mentality with which I could cope when I was confronted with it next morning in the aftermath of the 'flat tire landing' episode. But again, back to the sequence.

By the Grace of God we became airborne and were off into the night sky.

Frank, with his usual competence, had the course ready when asked, and we headed off to the French coast to pay a social call on the good folk at Bamiers to see if we couldn't persuade them to cease and desist sending their missiles to the jolly folk in London.

The night's trip was uneventful after we had left the English coast, and the Pathfinders were at their usual excellent best in their marking.

This was one of seven such sites attacked by seven hundred thirty-nine bombers, twenty-two of that were lost to the defences.

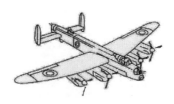

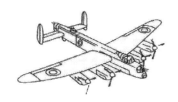

The Germans were counting heavily on this 'new' weapon, the buzz bomb', to help turn the tide of war in their favour, and had moved large numbers of searchlights and night fighters into the region to beef up the defences.

They had a clear moonlit night in that to do their work.

For some reason, that no one seemed to understand, all the bombers lost were Lancasters.

We arrive back at base and wait for all the other aircraft to land, and then ask for landing clearance only to be given the 'news' by the tower that we had a flat tire. We assured them that we knew, and again asked for landing clearance.

The tower then tells us proceed to the emergency landing aerodrome at Carnaby (about twenty minutes flying time away from Linton), so we suggest that we can land at Linton as well as we can land at Carnaby. But back comes the word that the wing commander has directed us to Carnaby. So away we go.

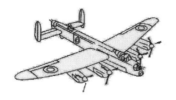

It is by now bright and sunny, and Larry and I plot our strategy to get this wounded bird back on the ground with the least possible damage.

We know that the right flat tire is going to be ripped off of the rim as soon as the weight of the plane comes down on it and the metal wheel rim is going to dig into the asphalt and swerve the aircraft to the right.

So we land the aircraft with the right wheel as close as possible to the edge of the runway, and as we slow down we swerve off the runway to the right, and are on the grass controlling the motion with brake and throttle, bringing the aircraft to a halt with a minimum roll forward.

Now it is gremlin time again, as swerving off the runway we are heading for one of the bomb blast shelters that have been built on the aerodrome. They are made of brick, about three or so feet tall and fifteen or so feet long.

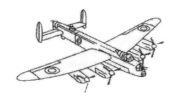

The sides have been covered to a slope with earth so any bomb blast will ride over the shelter and keep any damage to people lying in the shelter to a minimum.

As we come swerving off of the runway in our mighty Lancaster, in the direction of the shelter, we see a young airman and his airwoman girlfriend jump up out of the shelter and head hell for leather in the opposite direction. All the crew members were out watching the proceedings and it was just the splendid tension-breaker we needed to make our day.

We did have a great laugh as we waited for the ground crew to come out and join the party.

You don't have to be very imaginative to guess the comments that came from the crew members when they stopped laughing at the rapidly disappearing young lovers.

Perhaps the final comment was a borrowing from William Shakespeare who had once said, "That the course of true love never did run smooth". Forsooth and Gadzooks ! Indeed, war is hell. But again, back to the real world.

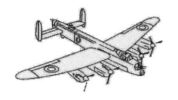

Thanks again to Larry, it was textbook landing. The tire was torn off, a small brake line hose was damaged, and we lost a gallon of brake fluid.

The ground crew was soon out with their equipment and, in about an hour, they had replaced the tire, the line, and topped off the brake fluid.

The aircraft was jacked up and we did a couple of retraction tests on the undercarriage, and, since all was well, we got permission to get back onto the runway and go back to Linton.

The Linton tower seemed surprised to see us but gave us permission to land.

I should point out that they had a standard procedure at Carnaby. They automatically sent a signal to the squadron headquarters of any aircraft that landed there, advising the aircraft owner what the status of the aircraft was so they could do the forward planning necessary.

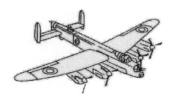

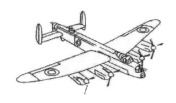

As luck would have it, there were two aircraft with the letter X designation. We were E L-X. The other X aircraft had been badly damaged and was a write-off. Now the little man who was responsible for sending these messages back to the individual squadrons had somehow gotten locked into this dance with the gremlins and sent a message to Linton that EL-X was a write-off and to the other squadron that their aircraft would be back shortly. All this was not known to us at the time.

We knew that the aircraft would have to be checked by the maintenance chappies so we parked down at their hangar instead of going to the dispersal. Then it's off to the Intelligence section to get de-briefed, and then breakfast and bedtime.

The Intelligence officer tells me that the wing commander wants to see me.

So the crew beetled off to breakfast while I went up to the office of the boss on the second storey of the hangar.

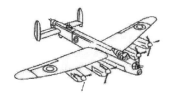

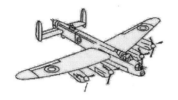

May I inject a personal note here that, at this point, I thought that the engineer and I had managed a rather creditable night's work with the takeoff and landing problem. Fool that I was.

The orderly room and its staff were outside his door on this warm summer's day, and I'm ushered in as soon as I appear.

As soon as the wing commander sees me, and with his office door wide open, he launches into a loud vulgar tirade about any "g d sob pilot who is stupid enough to write of an aircraft with a flat tire, and on, and on, and then, as he was about to run out of steam, he gave me hell for having hit the cedar palings around the beacon with my tire on takeoff.

When he finally ran out of steam, I told him that the aircraft was parked right in front of the hangar and if he cared to look out of the window, he could see it.

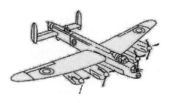

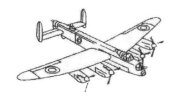

After a small pause he shouted at me, "That's all. Get out." Convinced that he had taken leave of his senses, I gladly did, and went off to join the crew at breakfast wondering what on earth was wrong with the wing commander.

The incident did not really serve to deepen the regard we held each other. It was only later that I was made aware of the mixed-up signals from Carnaby.

Four hours and fifty minutes flying time for the night.

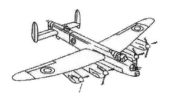

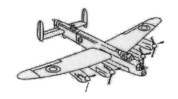

Foret-de Eavy
27/28 June 1944

Once again a very busy night for the Bomber Command, with one thousand forty-nine sorties out servicing the needs of the hard-pressed invasion forces on the ground below us.

Railway junctions and buzz-bomb sites were visited. Seven hundred twenty-one aircraft, including ours, were on the buzz-bomb sites.

Three aircraft were lost.

Three hours and thirty-five minutes flying time for the night.

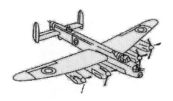

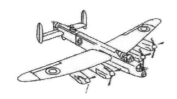

Criel
12 July, 1944

Two hundred twenty-two bombers were sent out to visit a huge fuel and ammunition dump the Germans had established.

Again we were visiting in daylight and there was some cloud cover, so the results were not clearly visible.

No aircraft were lost.

Four hours and thirty minutes flying for the trip.

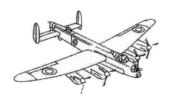

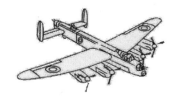

Caen
18 July, 1944

The Allied armies on the ground were vigorously pushing the Germans eastwards and had a significant number of German units bottled up near Caen where the escape avenues were restricted.

It was a major opportunity to get some very heavy firepower laid on the tanks and heavy weapons these units had, so nine hundred forty-two aircraft were sent out to bomb these units.

It was the first time that a strategic force of this kind had been used in this type of tactical support role.

Two German Panzer Division were badly mauled in this raid, and the armies below benefitted considerably from the confusion in the German organization.

Four hours and ten minutes flying time for our day's work.

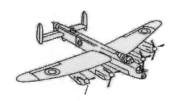

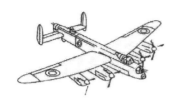

Wesseling
18/19 July, 1944

Back to our beloved Germany again. Only one hundred ninety-four bombers were targeted on this synthetic oil plant.

The fuel was, of course, vital for the German war effort. The Pathfinders were bang-on again in their marking of the target, and the raid was very successful. But, from our point of view it was another story.

The small number of bombers in the stream did not give us the protection from radar we were accustomed to, and the night fighters were all over us.

As we entered the target area, we were again picked up by radar and then instantly, we had about fifty searchlights on us and the flak devils not far behind.

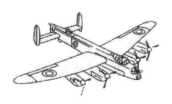

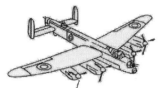

The fighters buzzing around looked as if we had stumbled into a bees' nest, and by the time we had shaken them off, we had lost some thousands of feet of altitude and had to get ourselves sorted out to get through a bombing run and make way for home.

On the way home, we were attacked by another fighter and although we had some bullet holes, nothing of consequence had been hit and all systems were still functioning.

Back to base and take our turn landing, and then to the briefing room. We were a sorry, dragged-out looking lot as we came into the briefing room and as soon as the Base Commander, Group Captain Clare Annis saw us, he came over and asked what had happened this time.

I should pause here for a word about this wonderful man. He would always be at the briefings for the night ops and would always be there when the crews came back helping in any and every way he could. He knew all the crews and made himself familiar with their work on the squadron.

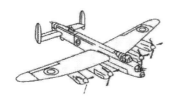

When we told him what had happened, he turned to our beloved squadron commander and said, "Surely this crew can be screened off the squadron". He said he thought we had used up all our luck and had had enough punishment for one tour. Since there was no shortage of new crews waiting, we would not be missed.

We then got our coffee and went to the debriefing. Next day the wing commander called me in and told me that we were finished our tour and to get the flying logbooks from the crew so they could be signed off and we could leave.

You won't be surprised to hear that we went out to the Alice Hawthorn pub and had a few beers that night. I recall Mike Nelligan, with his usual dry Irish wit, saying at one point in the evening, "Well, so much for the superstition about X-ray."

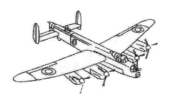

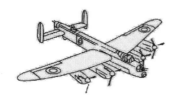

In a couple of days we were all gone from Linton. Frank, the navigator, left to be an instructor at the Navigation School at Abingdon, Larry, went on to instruct flight engineers at the school at Leeming, Mike went back to Canada, and I went to the 1695 Bomber Development Training Flight, at Dalton. This was the flight school that did the training work with the bombers. The Spitfires would get up into the sky and pretend to attack the bombers, who, in turn, would go into their evasive action routines to shake off the fighters.

The months I spent flying the Spitfires, Hurricanes, and Magisters seemed like a splendid fun-filled holiday. Most of the pilots on the unit were tour expired Fighter Command pilots, and you can imagine their comments when they were told that a 'truck driver' from a bomber squadron was going to join them.

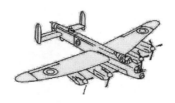

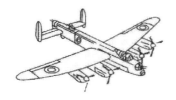

We stayed there until the end of the war was formally declared, and then went back to Canada aboard the Isle de France.

The British and the Canadians were gearing up to go to the Pacific theatre as the 'Tiger Force' (a new version of Bomber Command) and help the Americans win the war against the Japanese.

Before we could finish our disembarkation leave the two atomic bombs had completed the job and new directions were needed for all.

I've often thought of those days on the squadron and the many fine men who were lost. Many fine men of so much promise, all denied to their families and their countries.

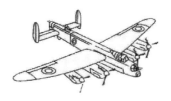

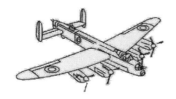

Nowhere have I seen a finer epitaph for them than in the Funeral Oration given by Pericles, the great Athenian leader. After one of the many battles between Sparta and Athens, as the dead soldiers were being brought into the Forum in Athens on their shields, as was the custom, he said,

> "But the man who can most truly
> be accounted brave is he who best
> knows the meaning of what is sweet
> in life and what is terrible, and then
> goes out undeterred to meet what is to come."

Such were the men of Bomber Command.

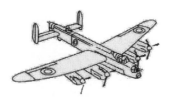

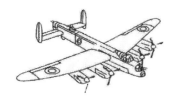

Time Out

It would not be seemly if I were to conclude these pages without an honest, up-front confession of the time I spent in 'jail' in Jolly Olde England.

But you need a bit of background. Buried as we were in the wilds of Yorkshire, one did not have the constant feeling that God and all His angels were about all the time, so one stoically went through life's routines hoping for salvation another day.

There were only about twenty of us pilots on the unit, and we had a flight tower controller who had been, I heard, told in a tarot card reading that he wold come to a sticky end when some mad pilot crashed into the tower. Whenever we would be out on exercises with the bombers and came back to base, if all was quiet in the circuit we would take a cut or two at the tower at about two hundred feet before we called in to ask for permission to land.

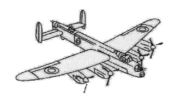

The first cut invariably brought friend Thomas running out onto the balcony that ran around the tower looking for the aircraft that might bring his doom.

He was then at least positioned to bail out over the balcony if need be.

We would by then be most of the way through our second cut and then roll over and come in to land.

This was a regular procedure that all but the most puritanical of pilots did and no one paid any attention to it, until the fateful day when two wing commanders from training command in Canada were visiting the unit.

They had fought a very difficult war in Canada and now, in these later days, needed to spend a few days in England so that they could ensure their grandchildren that "yes indeed war was hell'.

They had come up to Dishforth with the assurance that they could get a quick trip in a Spitfire and have this entry in their logbook to boast of back in the wilds of Training Command in Canada.

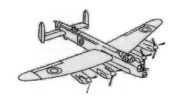

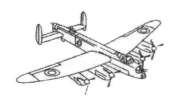

Of course such low flying in Training Command would get you an automatic court martial ipso facto where you are.

Now it just so happens that as I came back to take my first cut at the tower, our commanding officer, who is junior in rank to these two wing commanders, is sitting in the cockpit of a Spitfire. He has one wing commander on each wing beside him, explaining how one starts up and get airborne in a Spitfire.

You don't need the vision of an Old Testament prophet to guess at their reaction to my first, much less my second, cut.

Suffice it to say that as I parked my aircraft in one of the farther dispersals, draped my parachute over my shoulder and started back to the pilot's shack I was met half way by the adjutant who had a railway warrant in his hand for me to catch the afternoon train to Sheffield. When I protested he simply said "You may have a court martial if you insist" as he told me about the two visitors who had sealed my fate.

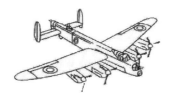

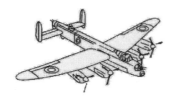

Lunch and packing were rather hurried activities so I could get a ride into town and the railway station. I grumbled mightily all the while. On board the train I met a nice young pilot from one of the other Canadian bases in Yorkshire, McAlpine by name, and we struck up a friendship when we discovered that we were both going to the same destination.

The same destination was the Air Crew Correction School known as ACCS. In years gone by, there had been a huge vehicle maintenance depot at Sheffield, but the vehicles were all somewhere in Europe engaged in the unpleasantness that was still proceeding there. There was a parking area there, that would have brought unending joy to any drill corporal's heart.

There were about 120 of us 'criminals' there - I had no idea how easy it was to sink so deeply into sin. The days were long, with an early morning   physical training session before breakfast, then an hour's drill and lectures until lunch.

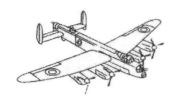

Each afternoon brought its own hour of drill and physical training before the dinner hour arrived, and then we were blessed with a couple of evening lectures and a 10 pm roll call. It was the sort of day that any pilot would find truly exciting.

We didn't do drill in the mass, but were broken up into groups of about twenty four, and then each of us were called out to take a turn acting as drill corporal.

The Sergeant Major was in charge, and duly noted on his pad how brilliant, or otherwise, our efforts were.

Strangely enough, after a couple of days everyone entered into the fun and for a few they actually recalled some of their earlier drill sessions. It didn't seem to matter how much drill you knew, but it was important to be heard, at least by the Sergeant Major.

And then, if you had been heard, instead of being truculent and bad-tempered about the drill, you would be placed on 'privileges', that meant that you did not have to go on evening lectures or be at roll call, and could go out of camp for the week-end days.

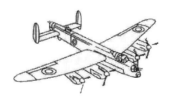

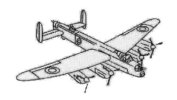

Sheffield was an iron and steel, heavy industry town that had had most of its menfolk drafted into the British military services early in the war, and as many of them as possible had been replaced by ladies from wherever they could be found.

So, in the fullness of time, as McAlpine and I found ourselves on 'privileges', we wandered downtown to find a pint or two of beer.

We came to a pub known as 'The Roundabout', with a large oval bar in the place and wall-to-wall girls who seemed all not to have had a date for the last two or three years. And there, as if we had died and gone to Heaven, were these two fools in blue, with a look of wonderment and disbelief on our faces.

We made our way to the bar and ordered a couple of pints, and, as we lit a cigarette I felt a tap on my shoulder, and looking around saw a pretty young lady who needed a light for her cigarette. Of course, my lighter came out again and then she thanked me most prettily and just stood there.

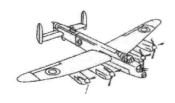

In about the same amount of time McAlpine had had the same treatment, and our two had suddenly become a foursome. After an awkward, quiet moment, we asked them if we could buy them a beer, and quickly got a breathless thank you.

I had hardly had a dip of my beak in my pint of beer when I got another tap on my shoulder - the other side - and there is another pretty young lady who needs a light for her cigarette.

Only a cad would not oblige, and, after she has her cigarette going, she joins the party.

The looks from the other two tell us that they do not like her muscling in, but she is with us. All are chatting us up as pretty as you please. Now this is as remote from the wilds of Yorkshire as you can get. We have about twenty officers on the base, a bunch of ground crew chappies, and three women working in the kitchen. We have scanned the horizon, in and out of our Spitfires, until our eyes were crossed, and nary a pretty girl was to be seen. And now they were wall-to-wall.

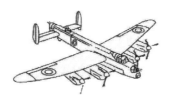

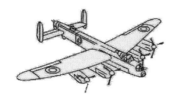

After a while McAlpine and I went to the men's room and his comments about how these ladies were more accurate and deadly on a target than any German night fighter he had ever seen, lingered long in my mind.

Soon after we returned it obviously was time to step up the attack; one of the young ladies tugged at my sleeve and as I looked at her, she whispered that she would like to speak to me privately. I stepped aside with her, and she then told me that she was just interested in my welfare, and that the other girl who had joined us was a prostitute.

I thanked her for her solicitude and we stepped back into the group.

Of course, it was not long before the other girl tugged at my sleeve and asked to speak to me privately, so I did and we did, and she whispered that she only wanted to protect me and told me that the other girl was a prostitute.

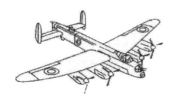

I was appropriately shocked, of course, and thanked her for her concern as we rejoined the group.

After a couple more beers, McAlpine and I retired to the men's room again, and after I recounted the story he surmised they might both be right, and perhaps we ought to find another pub to see if it was wall-to-wall girls as well.

After all, if you are in a bazaar you should examine all the goods before you decide to purchase.

We laughed later, recalling how we were furious at having been sent down to Sheffield, and then by the time we were at the end of our second of three weeks, we were wondering what we could do to get an extension on the course.

Alas, it was not to be, and with heavy hearts we went back to the bleak and barren Yorkshire moors.

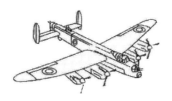

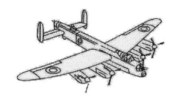

Monk's Habit
"There ain't nothin' like a dame".

How often the words from 'South Pacific' used to ricochet through my mind at the strangest of times. Here I was, deeply immersed in the world of philosophy and theology at the Pontifical Institute trying to forget the terrible days of World War Two.

This place was an oasis of peace and holy quiet in that one could gather one's soul together and think about a world with larger horizons and rather different values than I had found in the crucible of angst that my life as a bomber pilot had shaped for me.

Only two days earlier a number of us students had been walking down Bloor Street after a class, and, as we paused near a construction site for a red light to change, someone behind us started a jackhammer.

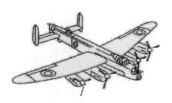

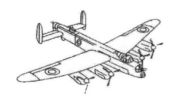

My reflex was instantaneous. All the others wondered what on earth I was doing on the ground. Had I taken leave of my senses? Had I tripped? Was I ill?

They didn't know that a jackhammer sounded exactly like a heavy machine gun firing close by. I had a lot of adjusting to do to become a member of this part of the human race again. Socratic dialogue can be as elegantly discursive as the afternoon will allow, but the sound of a machine gun firing, once learned, invited your earnest attention, 'tout de suite'!

But I digress. I haven't heard any guns firing since I left my temporary calling as a bomber pilot in the last great unpleasantness and I was mesmerized by the elegant logic of the philosophical and theological systems that were present to me each day as I took my place as a student in these hallowed halls.
The contrast was as startling and
often entered my mind as I went
to class or the library.

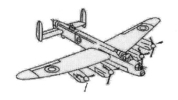

I realized I was an intruder in this school as I was not of the faith of the good folk who surrounded me in the dorm, in class and elsewhere, but no one missed me except at morning Mass.

I was careful not to intrude into classroom questions, time that I considered belonged to the other students - my questions to the professors came after class when I tracked one down over a cup of coffee in the Tuck Shop.

All of my heathen propensities could hang out at a time like this, and usually did. But they were unimaginably generous with their time and tolerant of my questions. The undergraduate days were gone and the in-depth pursuits were the order of the day.

One day, while going over some of the observations of St. Augustine in the library, I was hit in a most forceful way with a searing memory. It was as if someone had torn a deep scar off of my soul and brought to light a long-repressed memory of the real reason I had been born.

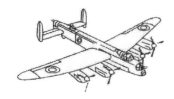

The savage hurt was once more so palpable I could not stop the tears that ran down my cheeks onto the papers on the table.

It took a few moments before I realized that all eyes in the room focused on me and I rose and stumbled out of the library and went back to my room in the dorm.

I cannot imagine how long it took me to stop the convulsive tears and agony that welled up out of the so long-repressed memory of the day my life was destroyed in the winter of 1943.

It was as if I had been caught up in a process that was beyond my control and I was a simple instrument in projecting this truth into the psyche of those who were around me, no matter how uncomprehending they might be.

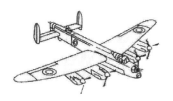

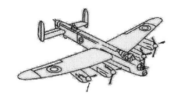

I can vividly recall the agony of reliving that dreadful moment that had destroyed my life. How could I describe what I was feeling? No simple words could do this, but was there some process by that I could tell these people what had happened to destroy me so completely?

The monk's habit that I had been imperceptibly stitching around my psyche in the last three years, piece by piece, was suddenly rent apart.

The vision of the girl with the red, red hair flashed again across the farthest reaches of my memory.

I cannot recall the writing of the words, but the substance was always vividly engraved on the walls of the deepest caverns of my soul.

In any case, when one of my concerned friends came to knock on my door he found me with this poem in my hand. I had no notion of the passage of time, but I knew that I had spoken a prayer of thanks for what I had once had, to a kindly God.

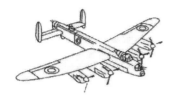

I thanked my friend for his concern and assured him that I was all right and just getting the memories sorted out so they could be lived with for all the barren years to come.

I had now described the beginning and the end of the love story buried for so long in the deepest regions of my heart. But there had been more - the dazzling two weeks when my life had really begun.

The memories flooded out easily and took their shape in my mind, and then seemed almost to flow out as if I were nothing more than a passive instrument of recording, responding to a stimulus from some unseen source.

The sequence was simple, but how could one ever find words to cast the spell on the reader's mind as it has been emblazoned on my heart. I only knew I must try.

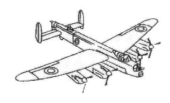

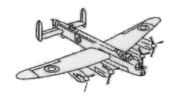

The Girl with the Red Red Hair

The sea breeze was fair and blew through her
hair,
As we walked barefoot on the water-shaded sand,
This was our first date, she'd met me at the gate,
"Let's go to my favourite place" and shyly took my
    hand.

I was deeply drunk with the beauty of her eyes
and the red, red hair,
My tongue could find no words to speak, they
were all shining in my eyes,
The day was blue -sky perfect, cotton-wool clouds
and screaming gulls,
As she told me of her family, and of her life on the
isle of Skye.

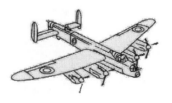

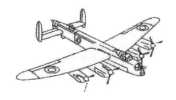

She said that she'd been waiting for me, a long, long
   time it seemed,
   And how she just knew, when she first saw me, at
the tea dance weeks ago,
   Then, how in her heart, she laughed at me for
trying to avoid a kindly fate,
   For the woven threads of destiny had linked us, in
a way that we could not forgo.

She knew what I was, my uniform told her all she
   needed to know.
   How it took some days to understand why I was
     frightened of her so
   She laughed at my fears and my picture of her in
     widow's weeds,
   Said the threads of destiny had woven the path
that we must go.

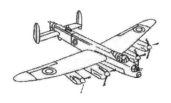

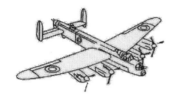

When I asked her how could the culture of the windy Isle of Skye

Embrace a raw-boned lad from the spaces of Canada's wide, wide west,

She stopped and touched my face, then gave me our first kiss

And said," When a heart is full of love it always does know best."

"The things that we did learn, in growing up, were just a cultural accretion,

Peripheral to a loving heart, not at the core of what life's about,

That two in love could make a home, each focused on the giving,

When a heart with love does overflow there's never any doubt."

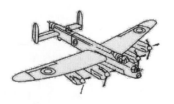

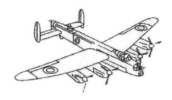

And so she brought into my life this incandescent,
    meteoric vision
Of love and life and destiny, horizons constantly
    expanding
Beyond my focus of the war and my mighty flying
    bomber.
The love and beauty of this girl my happy heart
    commanding.

With sea-air freshened appetites we made us a
small dinner,
And talked before a flickering fire, my churlish
fears to banish,
The exquisite beauty of her face, the sparkling
intellect,
It seemed a dream I dared not touch for fear the
dream would vanish.

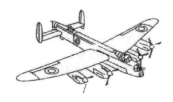

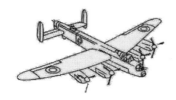

And oh! how the dream did vanish, but not just yet,
  And after a while she spoke of how my occupation
  For longevity had rather a poor reputation, or so she'd heard
  "We've waited these long empty years." There was no hesitation.

  As we awoke the sun-drenched skies caressed our eyes,
  And I had touched my dream, and yet it did not vanish,
  Her red, red hair blazed like a flickering Viking flame
  And I, a moth, that only death could banish.

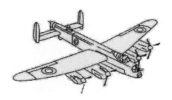

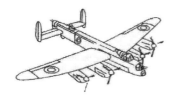

We loved and played, laughed the joyous days away,

Forgot time until the fateful day, when duty once more beckoned.

She said we'd marry when next I came, my tour of duty   ended,

And our life together would carry on, no ending could be reckoned.

She said when I had finished with this dreadful
        slaughter,
We'd have a cottage, rose bushes too, a nest that we could share,
And then she would make for me a splendid little
        daughter
Who would smile at me with her greenish eyes
        beneath her red, red hair.

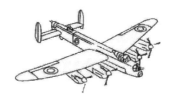

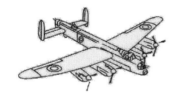

You

When first I looked at her I thought such
beauty could nor be,
So I looked away, until another day, and there
once more was she,
Who gathered my soul into her own with just a
single glance.
With just a trace of an elfin smile she set my
heat to dance.

But I was a stranger in a far off land, no future
could I see,
For I was a bomber pilot, no one would place
odds on me,
To fly and live, and have a life to give, to the
beautiful girl
Whose red, red hair and
bright green eyes did set my heart
awhirl.

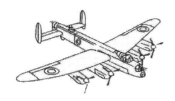

I was a boy from the farmlands in Canada's wide, side west,
All unaccustomed to the ways that the Britishers know best,
My silence and my distance, my protection they would be,
For wrapped in my coat of distance I always would be free.

And then, one day, in her fine English way, she asked me to a dance.
The green eyes looked into mine, I was utterly lost in her glance,
And we moved as one, a single heartbeat begun, the beat of a one true love
The blending of two souls in time, so rarely sent from Heaven above.

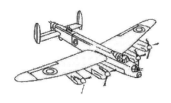

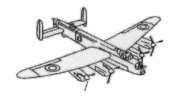

When first her hand touched mine it ignited a passionate flame,

To make this beautiful woman my own, I didn't yet know her name,

But I knew that this was the beginning of all that love could ever be,

We spoke not a word, we just danced on, in a heart-beat symphony,

A oneness in time, you could not imagine a bliss so sublime,

Or that God could create such a wonder as her love and mine.

But I had a vision of her in widow's weeds as I flew into the night,

It was a dark spectre that haunted me on every single flight,

But through the searchlights, the flak, the night fighters too,

Her face was the vision that
carried me through.

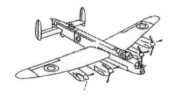

Time for some leave, I have two weeks in
hand,
I'll go to see her, we'll walk barefoot in the
sand,
The train leaves at two, arrives there at four,
 A five minute bus ride and I'll be at her door.

The bus stops. My heart stops. My brain reels
 at   the   sight,
Enemy bombers have levelled her house in the
        night.
 Of my vision of joy I'm suddenly bereft, there is
        nothing left,
Only a lifetime of sadness, gone is my heart's
        gladness. I wept.

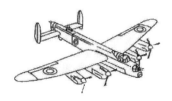

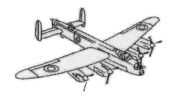

I managed to put a patch on the scarred rupture in my emotions and set about trying to stitch up the rent in the monk's habit that I had woven around my mind, but somehow the stitches would not hold.

The sight of a red-haired woman on the street or a walk on a sandy beach, and I could feel those stitches begin to pop as my mind and memory pushed through the confines of my monk's habit, as I was trying to reach for a bit of the world that had once been mine.

It was never within the reach of my extended heart or hand, of course, but some months later, when I found myself flying one of a new generation of jet airplanes, I would sometimes play tag with the cotton-wool clouds and imagine that the girl with the red, red hair was enjoying the game with me.

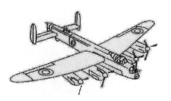

Wally's Poems

Poetry is the response of our innermost being to the ecstasy, the agony and the all-embracing mystery of life. It is a song, or a sigh, or a cry, often all of them together.
--Charles Angoff (Lerner, 1994)

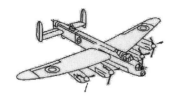

Tomorrows

They gave all of their tomorrows
So that your tomorrows could be free
Asking only that in your tomorrows
Lovingly remembered they would be.

What gifts have been found in your
tomorrows
That have been paid for with their lives,
The lilting laughter of your happy children
And the warm caresses of your wives.

These and a thousand others filled your
days
And filled your years.
Many joys and a few sorrows;
A land alive with
opportunity; their gift to
you
Paid for by giving
us all of their
 tomorrows.

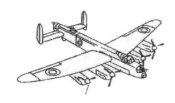

Their watchword was FOR FREEDOM
     and FREEDOM was their greatest gift to you,
        To live your life as you would have it be,
        And do the things that they could never do.

So bow your head and heart in prayerful thanks,
        Keep evergreen the thought so true,
        The memory of the courage and devotion
        That sent them out to fight and die for you.

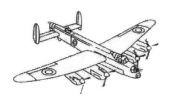

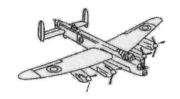

The Motley Crew

It was crewing day back at the OTU,
Time to select some buddies and form a crew,
Pilot, Nav, Bomb Aimer, and a gunner too,
Then try to shape 'em up to see if they will do.

We been cruising around, clearing in all day,
Now we're shovelled together down in hangar A,
Twenty pilots, nav's, and all the others too,
Chat each other up, see if you can form a crew.

They had some barrels of beer, sandwiches too,
I'm lost. Can a good nav hoist ten pints or two?
Now choosing a crew in this hullabaloo
Is the strangest damn thing I ever had to do..

So I drew another pint of this
splendid brew,
To reflect on this process of the
do-si-do
And ask myself where was it
going to go.

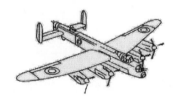

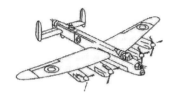

How could I measure anyone from where I stood?
Or conversely, would anyone think I could
Take 'em through a tour? Their lives and mine
Would, in a couple of months, be on the line.

There were no answers to be found by me,
My future was controlled by an unknown destiny,
As I finished my pint and went back to see,
But I wished I was fishing on the Miramichi.

I'd been out there longer than I thought I'd do
Everyone had scrambled to get into a crew,
And off in a corner, over on the far side
Were the left over chaps, and they became my pride.

We're all packaged in blue, so you don't know,
If he's good or bad, how long it will take to show,
It's only when we're up there in
the skies
Will we know if this is a team or
just some guys.

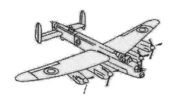

So I said You look like money in the bank,
Can I get in and fill in the blank?
We shook hands all around, then had another brew,
Next day we set out to see what this gang could do.

Circuits and bumps, cross countries galore,
Daytime, night time, then do some more,
There are dinghy drills and fighter affils
Till you have a fine tuned meshing of all the skills.

One night, from the Orkneys were homeward bound,
All was quiet, there's only the engines sound,
We're jumped by a German night fighter out to see
If we are a good target of opportunity.

But a sharp eyed gunner had the fellow in sight;
Soon his tracer shoots by in the dark of night,
We're up on a wing while he's
down below,
So he abandons us and then
home we go.

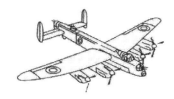

It was a sharp lesson we never forgot,
Not yet on the squadron and nearly got shot
Right out of the sky. It is a serious thing we do
And it meshes us together as the motley crew.

A couple more weeks and we'll be squadron bound
Leaving this place where we first found
That few things focus your mind as bullets do
When they're aimed right at your motley crew.

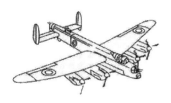

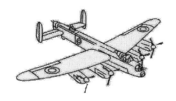

Requiem for a 408 Squadron Airman

In Flanders fields the poppies blow
Between the crosses, row on row,
That mark our place...”
          John McCrae.   In Flanders Fields

The nation sends its sons once more
To fight for freedom on a foreign shore,
They fly into the dark night sky
To bomb their target, and, perhaps, to
die.
These airmen had no time to see
The graves of their paternity,
In Flanders fields, or otherwise,
Before they died in the dark night skies.

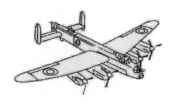

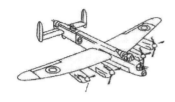

The briefing's done its time to go,
 We're off to Essen to see the show,
  And take a load of a nasty surprise,
   To drop it out of the dark night skies.
            Round and round the fighters go
            Searching for the Lancs below.

Runways behind us in the evening light,
 The Dutch coast ahead, but out of sight,
  To get to our maximum height we try
   Before we enter the dark night sky.
            Round and round the searchlights
            ply
            Seeking victims in the dark night sky.

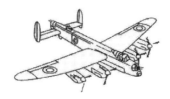

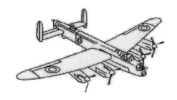

A change of course and we're running down
 To Happy Valley and old Essen town,
  Where the fighters, flak and searchlights rise
   To welcome us in the dark night skies.
    Round and round the flak does fly
    Seeking to kill in the dark night sky.

The target's marked, bomb run to go,
 Bombers silhouetted by the lights below,
  We're sitting ducks for a fighter's sharp eyes,
   He'll bring us death in the dark night skies.
    Round and round does the radar creep
    Snaring airmen's lives in its yellow
    sweep.

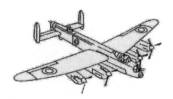

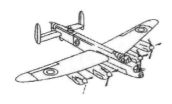

As the bomb doors close we're up on a wing,
 Turning away from this horrid thing,
  Down to the right and on a quick rise,
   To get the hell away in the dark night skies
           Round and round the fighters go,
           Searching for the Lancs below.

Outward bound and pick up your track,
 Only the gunners can look back,
  No time to relax they well realize,
   Death awaits them still in the dark night skies.
           Round and round the flak does fly,
            Seeking to kill in the dark night sky.

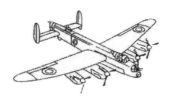

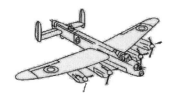

"Heads Up" now, we're homeward bound,
  Keep a sharp lookout, fighters still abound,
    There's a hose of tracer right before your eyes,
    And someone has died in the dark night skies.
**Round and round does the radar creep,
Snaring airmen's lives in its yellow
sweep.**

At Runnymede their names are found,
They have no place in hallowed ground,
They fought their battle in the sky
And bravely for us they did die.
No Taps or Reveille for them will play,
The Gods of War will have their way;
But the dark will fade as the sun does rise
When there is no terror in the dark night skies.

There are no crosses, row on row,
No poppies o'er these heroes
blow.

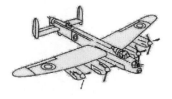

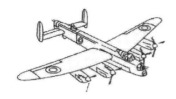

Sounds of the Heart

The gently creeping fingers of the early morning light
 Do probe down through the broken clouds
                        that have sheltered us this night,
As homeward we do make our weary way
                        from our sad duty done,
We've been to bomb the enemy in ancient Munich town.

A large break in the clouds gives us a pillar of sunlight.
I revel in the greening farms that push against the ocean bright,
And here and there we pass a windmill,
                        Its flails seeming to salute,
This noisy, ghostly bomber flying by, one of its engines mute.

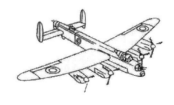

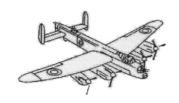

We've traded all our height for speed,
                      and now will hug the earth,
And hope that all the German fighters are
        out of gas and sleeping, each one in its berth,
We cross the coast, heading for home,
      an easy target, a wounded bird, low upon the sea,
For any German fighter who might still be out,
                    searching for a target of opportunity.

The wireless op, a peerless chap, has the
Woodbridge beacon bearing
              ready on demand,
The English coast is now in sight,
            how welcome is the sight of land,

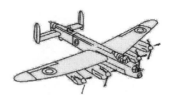

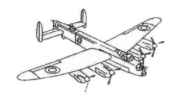

Woodbridge tower "X-ray, cleared straight in, runway right,"
"We have two wounded men on board", "All services are ready
you're the last ones in tonight".

My heart is full of tears for these two comrades true,
the medics now do have them, to do what they can do,
They're now in better hands than mine,
But none will have more prayers than I, my friends, for you.

Now, in a silent moment, methinks the sound that I did hear,
Was not the echo of a bomb burst, but the gentle knocking
of free men, on the door of Liberty.

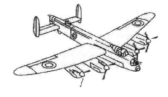

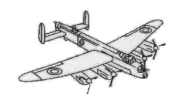

The 408 Squadron Ground Crew

Again the evening dusk doth deepen into dark
As the weary ground crew leave the aircraft, in its dispersal park,
They've laboured here since the early light of dawn,
And soon the laden aircraft, once more, into the night are gone.

They've laboured here, day long, to patch each wounded plane,
That returned to base in early morn, so it may fly again
This night, and carry forth its dreaded load of fearful death,
Perhaps, to be delivered with the aircrew men's last breath.

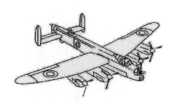

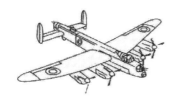

These ground crew, whose devotion to their plane does surely show,

Do labour here each day, in rain or shine, in sleet, in hail or snow;

They've seen so man of the air crews, as at night they do depart,

And in the morn they find a bleak dispersal, their's with a tearful, aching heart.

Betimes they see a young wife, now, in her widow's weeds,

Such a sorry payment for her husband's gallant deeds,

The war had called him forth, and to this place he'd bravely come,

One of the very many, who, to the   German fury did succumb.

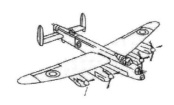

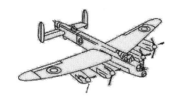

There were so very many, year over year, each name on name,

Who had helped to build this squadron's fearsome fame,

To tell of the tons delivered, of the many targets struck,

And of death, sometimes avoided, by a great, good stroke of luck.

And how these good, ground crew men would revel in the knowing,

That the aircrew's tour was over and now they are homeward going,

No one did count the endless, devoted hours these good ground crew did give

To ensure each plane was perfect so that the aircrew might just live.

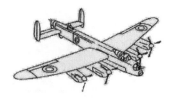

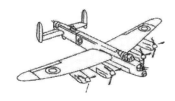

So these fine ground crew worked each day of every season,
Proud unsung heroes that they were, and proud with much good reason,
    They did a splendid job, with peerless work in every situation,
    Stand tall, good men, and take the 'Thanks' of aircrew and your nation.

    But most of all, while you stand tall, the air crews get the glory,
    For they are in the sky while bullets fly, and so the end of story,
        But they do know, as you do know, for even the best aircrew,
            Without your skills, devotion too, no aircraft ever flew.

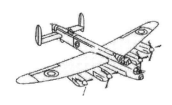

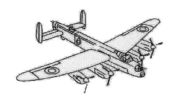

Taps

The sound of TAPS does ring the eerie silence
round,
  This gathered group, that doleful Death has found
  Beside this grave, to bid a haunting, last farewell
  To one they knew, and loved, so very, very well.

So young, bright spirit, born to fly and soar,
  You so enjoyed the splendid things that you will do
no more,
  No falcon, eagle ever reached your breathtaking
heights
  Or ever equaled the manoeuvres of your fantastic
flights.

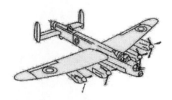

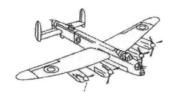

But now the sky is silent and there is no engine's roar,
       The earth begins to fall upon this pilot, who will fly no more,
              The bugle sound does softly echo round and round,
       And in this solemn gathering no dry eye can be found.

But as the bugle notes fall slowly from the sky, there is a cry,
       An eagle swoops, and in his flight does silently pass by,
    And then, before their eyes, he quickly climbs way out of sight
As if he was an escort, come to see an eagle's spirit homeward flight.

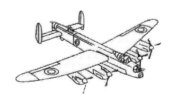

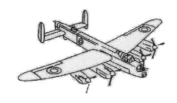

We had you for so short a time, so talented and bright,

Now you've gone, each heart is darkened by a touch of lonely night,

We'll have to wait, however long, to meet another time,

But in between, your memory will make our spirits climb.

The cherished memories of bright-eyed, antic wit,

The eager, happy grasp of each complicated bit

Of every field of study you conquered on your way

Then you received your pilot's wings, for you, the greatest day.

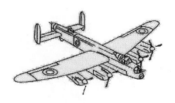

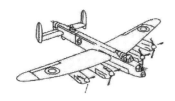

The echoes of the sounds of Taps still linger in our minds,

Your day has closed, now comes the peace your spirit finds,

Our reverie is broken by the trumpet's clarion call,

And Reveille announces that you are waiting for us all.

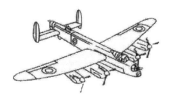

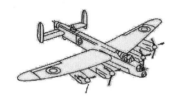

Squadron Echoes

Sometimes, in the darkness of a quiet night,
Will come some remembered sound or sight
Of the days and nights of a dark and distant
past
When 408 did send its bombers to do their ugly
task.

The laden aircraft are climbing into the dusky sky,
On the ground the fading sound does echo all round.
And we, who are left here, in this empty place,
Will brace our hearts and minds, the morrow for to
face.

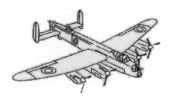

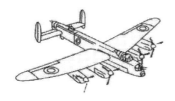

The aircrew in those bombers now do make their noisy way
Into the aerial trenches, placed to trap them as they may,
And the fury of the enemy will blaze with shot and shell
As they enter ever deeper into this special place in hell.

With bated breath the German fury waits to take its toll,
Of the bomber stream as it must to the target roll,
The searchlights, flak, night fighters too, will deal their share
Of death, and destruction, as the battle rages in the air.

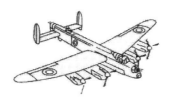

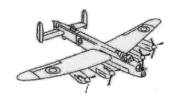

The first crack of dawn will penetrate the peaceful Yorkshire sky,
As the returning bombers, from their doleful errand, homeward fly,
 And as each haggard crew does take its weary place
 The status board reveals the name of every missing face.

'We regret to inform you"
Comes the message to his wife,
And then begins the flow of tears
That will echo through her life.
930 times did "we" regret to inform "you",
That we had lost another comrade,
An airman, who bravely did his duty do,
And in the
doing, gave
his life for
you.

184

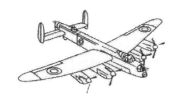

An Old Love and a New

When I said "Goodbye" to my Lancaster bird,
It was a tearful farewell, though I said not a
word,
Through my mind went the many times she
and I
Had played the deadly game of dicing in the
dark night sky.

The night the searchlights had caught us over
old Berlin town,
The fighters, like a swarm of bees, trying to
shoot us down,
She's still got the bomb load and lots of gas in
the tanks,
I'm blinded by searchlights, but she takes the
turns and the banks;
We're jinking like crazy to
left and to the right,
Climbing and diving,
changing speed and our height,

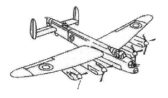

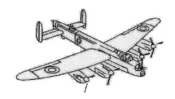

With all this weight on board she should have fallen apart

But she knew that we loved her, and held us close to her   heart.

We've gone from twenty to eight thousand feet in this game

The lights now have lost us, the fighters the same,

Then we turn back to drop our bombs, that is why we came.

This Lancaster - old X-ray - was the queen of the skies,

Had so much love lavished on her by all those great ground   crew guys,

They patched up the holes that the aircrew brought back,

And kept her at the ready for another attack.

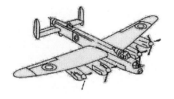

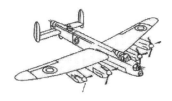

And now each of the crew goes his separate way,
  These comrades who served with you day after day,
  Each of you fine-tuned to deal with that war in the sky,
  Each giving all, each depending on all, and now its Goodbye.

  And now I'm looking at this Spitfire girl,
  She'll take me upstairs and give me a whirl,
  And I'll fall in love again, how could I deny
  The embrace of this beauty, the fire in her eye;

  But still I'll keep a part of my heart for old X-ray alone,
  And that splendid crew of mine, finer men are not known,
  They have faced, with me, the worst that the enemy could give,
  And each has trusted each, gave their all, so that all could live,

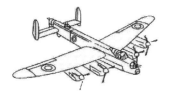

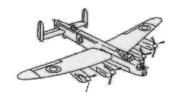

Those splendid men who dared with me, to face the dark uncertainty

    Each night would bring; and shared with me their constancy

    To see a duty was well done; and we, now that the tour is through

    Each will go his separate way.

    But the bonds are forged and they will stay,

    Forged in the crucible of death and danger, strengthened day by day.

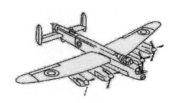

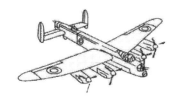

High Flight

Oh! I have slipped the surly bonds of earth, And
danced the skies on laughter-silvered wings;
Sunward I've climbed, and joined the tumbling
mirth
Of sun-split clouds, --and done a hundred things
You have not dreamed of --Wheeled and soared
and swung
High in the sunlit silence. Hov'ring there
I've chased the shouting wind along, and flung My
eager craft through footless halls of air... Up, up
the long, delirious, burning blue
I've topped the wind-swept heights with easy
grace
Where never lark or even eagle flew --
And, while with silent lifting mind I've trod
The high untrespassed sanctity
of space,
Put out my hand, and touched
the face of God.

John Gillespie Magee Jr.

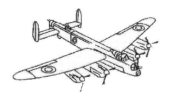

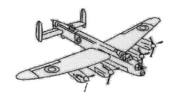

Throughout our lifetimes, come what may, each man will say

     The heady wine of danger has lingered long with me; one may

     Forget so much, but this is mine until my dying day.

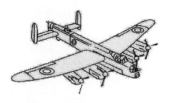

Made in the USA
San Bernardino, CA
21 August 2014